Bengalis in London's East End

Researched, compiled & edited
by

Ansar Ahmed Ullah & John Eversley

Supported by
The National Lottery®
through the Heritage Lottery Fund

heritage
lottery fund

স্বাধীনতা ট্রাস্ট

ppre

LONDON
metropolitan
university

Training provided by
London Metropolitan University

BISHOPSGATE
INSTITUTE partly supported by

Published by the Swadhinata Trust
70 Brick Lane (1st floor), London E1 6RL. UK

www.swadhinata.org.uk

Funded by the Heritage Lottery Fund

Researched compiled and edited by
Ansar Ahmed Ullah & John Eversley

Edited by
Jenny Vaughan, Julia Bard and David Rosenberg

Research volunteers
Alice Flight, Fatima Luna, Hemayet Hossain and
Lovely Khanom.

Project Management Group
Ansar Ahmed Ullah, *Project Manger (Swadhinata Trust)*
Julie Begum, *Secretary (Swadhinata Trust)*
John Eversley, *Project Supervisor, Senior Lecturer,*
Department of Applied Social Sciences, London Metropolitan University

Designed & printed by Fairkey
www.fairkey.co.uk

Cover photograph - Lascars at the Opening of the Tower Hill Memorial in 1928
(Photo by Fox Photos/Getty Images)

ISBN 978-0-9565745-0-3

Credits and Acknowledgements

Photographs

The authors and publisher would like to thank the following for permission to use their photographs in this book: Ansar Ahmed Ullah/Swadhinata Trust, Ashraf Mahmud Neswar, Altyerre, Alan Dein, Bengali Christian Fellowship Bishopsgate Institute, Bethnal Green Photo Archive, Blackwall pictures, British Library Board, City of Westminster Archives, Cinema Theatre Association Archive, Dishari Shilpi Goshti, East End Community School, Fox Photos/Getty Images, Hackney Archives, Hindu Temple in Rhondda Grove, Imperial War Museum, Janomot, Julie Begum, Ken Russell, Kois Miah, London Borough of Enfield, London Metropolitan Archives, Lovely Khanom/Swadhinata Trust, Mitali Housing Association, Mohiuddin Siddique, Museum of London, National Portrait Gallery, Paul Trevor, PNA Rota/Getty Images, Ragged School Museum, Royal Geographical Society with IBG, Sanaton Association, Sherwan Chowdhury, Shiv Banerjee, Syeda Lovely Choudhury, Syed Abdul Kadir, Taj Stores, Time Life Pictures/Getty Images, Tower Hamlets Homeless Campaign and Tower Hamlets Local History Library and Archives.

Mohiuddin Siddique of Eyeculture scanned, reproduced and printed some of the old photographs.

Text

The authors have drawn extensively on the work of the following people and we would like to thank them and their publishers for permission to use passages from their work.
We have not only used passages from the work of the authors below but we have also benefited greatly from their inspiration and in many cases friendship.

C. Adams, for passages from Across Seven Seas and Thirteen Rivers (1994) found on pages 21, 47 and 48

British Library: Help for Researchers: Asians in Britain: Ayahs, Servants and Sailors Marine Department Records [online] for passages reproduced on pages 27, 43, and 46

The Old Bailey for passage from The Proceedings of the Old Bailey, 1674-1913 quoted in Moving Here, Tracing your roots [online] reproduced on page 30

Y. Choudhury, for passage from The Roots and Tales of the Bangladeshi Settlers (1993), reproduced on page 21

Robins, N. 2006. The Corporation That Changed the World: How the East India Company Shaped the Modern Multinational. London. Pluto Press reproduced on...

R. Taylor for passage from Walks Through History: Exploring East End (2004), reproduced on page 103

Tower Hamlets History online for passage on page 7

R. Visram, for passages from Ayahs, Lascars and Princes: Indians in Britain 1700-1947 (1986), reproduced on page 23

R. Visram, for passage from Asians in Britain – 400 years of History (2002), reproduced on page 9

G. Wemyss for passage from White Memories, White Belonging: Competing Colonial Anniversaries in 'Postcolonial' East London (2008), reproduced on page 15

Research & other assistance

Abdul Quayum Khalique (Jamal), *Taj Stores*
Abdul Shahid, *Swadhinata Trust*
Abu Taher, *Shanghati Literary Society*
Ashraf Mahmud Neswar, *Manager, Kobi Nazrul Centre*
Alice Bigelow, *Arts & Community consultant*
Andy Simons, *Modern British Collections/Social History, The British Library*
Auste Mickunaite, *Permissions, The British Library*
Claire Renard, *Grants Assistant, London Team, Heritage Lottery Fund*
Abul Azad, *Surma Project Worker, Toynbee Hall*
Amanda Sebestyen, *writer & activist*
Alice Sielle, *Belief in Bow, St Barnabas Church*
Bilkis Begum Mosoddik, *Swadhinata Trust*
Biplob & Shahed *of Fairkey*
Brian Oakaby, *GLA*
Cath Richardson, *Grants Assistant, London Team, Heritage Lottery Fund*
Chila Burman, *Artist*
Christopher Lloyd, *Local Studies Officer, Tower Hamlets Local History Library and Archives*
Chris Rawlings, *Picture Library, The British Library*
Clive Polden, *Cinema Theatre Association Archive*
Cllr Shafi Khan, *Croydon*
Cllr Sherwan Chowdhury, *Croydon*
Dan Jones, *author of Exploring Banglatown and the Bengali East End*
Daniele Lamarche, *author of Bengalis in East London*
David Parry, *Acquisitions Curator, Photograph Archive, Imperial War Museum*
Dr. Tom Wareham FRSA, *Curator of Maritime and Community Histories, Museum of London Docklands*
Dr. Jennifer Howes, *Curator, Prints Drawings & Photographs, Asia Pacific & Africa Collections, The British Library*
David Bell, *Image Sales & Licensing, Imperial War Museum*
Dilip Roy, *General Secretary, Hindu Temple in Rhondda Grove*
Edgar Aromin, *Admin Assistant - Photograph Archive, Image Sales Licensing, Imperial War Museum*
Elizabeth Pinel, *Schools and Community Learning Manager, Bishopsgate Institute*
Emma Butterfield, *Picture Librarian, Rights & Images, National Portrait Gallery*
Ed Weech, *Deputy Library Manager, Bishopsgate Institute*
Emma Dakin, *Library Assistant, Bishopsgate Institute*
Erica Davies, *Ragged School Museum*
Faruque Ahmed, *Author & researcher*
Felix Gott, *Grants Assistant, Heritage Lottery Fund - London Team*
Fiona Cormack, *Library and Archive Assistant, Museum of London*
Georgie Wemyss, *author of White Memories, White Belonging: Competing Colonial Anniversaries in 'Postcolonial' East London*
Graham Fisher, *Chief Executive, Toynbee Hall*
Hasnat Chowdhury, *Walworth Community & Enforcement, London Borough of Southwark*
Ian Kikuchi, *Assistant Curator, Film and Video Archive, Imperial War Museum*
Jamie Owen, *Picture Library Manager. Royal Geographical Society with IBG*
Jamil Iqbal, *Swadhinata Trust*
James Swapan Peris, *Bengali Christian Fellowship*
Jan Pimblett, *Principal Interpretation Officer, London Metropolitan Archives*
Jeremy Smith, *Assistant Librarian, London Metropolitan Archives*
Julia Rose, *Grants Officer, Heritage Lottery Fund - London team*
Jo Parker, *Archivist, Waltham Forest Archives*

Joan Casey, *Trinity House*
Ken Russell, *photographer*
K R Choudhury, *relative of Indian Labour leader Aftab Ali*
Kajal Sarker, *Bengali Christian Fellowship*
Kate Maconachy, *Getty images*
Kois Miah, *Photographer*
Lynn Harris, *Trinity House*
Maher Anjum, *Swadhinata Trust*
Malcolm Barr-Hamilton, *Borough Archivist, Tower Hamlets Local History Library and Archives*
Martin Mintz, *Picture Library Assistant, The British Library*
Maureen Roberts, *Interpretation Officer, City of London: London Metropolitan Archives*
Michael H. Fisher, *Danforth Professor of History, Oberlin College*
M A Rauf, *author of Londoner Smriti*
Matthew Pegler, *Director, Altyerre*
Mrinal Sarkar, *Sanaton Association*
Mohammed Osman Gani, *Brick Lane Trust*
Mogol Shomraht, *Deshi Movement*
Nighat Taimuri, *Development Officer, Heritage Lottery Fund*
Nikki Braunton, *Picture Library Researcher, Retail and Licensing, Museum of London*
Nick Robins, *author of The Corporation That Changed the World: How the East India Company Shaped the Modern Multinational*
Nurul Islam, *author of Probashir Kotha*
Olga Aleksandrova, *Volunteer*
Peter Ashan, *Learning and Outreach Officer, Waltham Forest Council's Museum, Gallery and Archives Service*
Prof Muhammad Nurul Huque, *East End Community School*
Rory Lalwan, *Senior Archives Assistant, City of Westminster Archives Centre*
Rozina Visram, *author of Ayahs, Lascars and Princes: Indians in Britain 1700-1947*
Sara Wajid, *Museum of London*
Sajjad Miah, *Brick Lane Mosque*
Sean Carey, *Centre for Research on Nationalism, Ethnicity and Multiculturalism (CRONEM), Roehampton University*
Siân Mogridge, *Archivist, Hackney Archives*
Sister Christine Croft
Shiv Banerjee, *retired sea captain*
Shofique Miah, *Mitali Housing Association*
Shompa Lahiri, *Centre for the Study of Migration at Queen Mary*
Suzanne Bardgett, *Head of Department of Holocaust and Genocide History, Imperial War Museum*
Syed Abdul Kadir, *retired marine engineer*
Stefan Dickers, *Library and Archives Manager, Bishopsgate Institute*
Stephanie Dacres, *Administration Manager, Bishopsgate Institute*
Uchchall Salique, *Dishari Shilpi Ghosti*
Vandana Patel, *Project Co-ordinator, Royal Geographical Society with IBG*
Yasmin Sultana Uddin, *Volunteer*
Yvonne Oliver, *Image Sales & Licensing, Imperial War Museum*
Uday Shankar Das, *Cultural activist*

Glossary

Ayahs	*Maids/nannies*
Bengali	*Racial – ethnic identity*
Bangladeshi	*Nationality – citizens of Bangladesh*
Baishakhi Mela	*Bengali New Year festival*
Banglatown	*Area surrounding Brick Lane*
Cheder	*Religious school for Jewish Children*
Donkeywallahs	*Bengali sailors who worked on the 'donkey engines' of a ship*
Jahajis	*Informal Bengali term for sailors*
Lascars	*From the Persian Lashkar, meaning 'military camp', and 'al-askar', the Omani word for a guard or soldier. Referred to Asian sailors*
Mirza	*Title given by emperor meaning commander or leader*
Mughals	*Mughal Emperors, descendants of the Timurids, were rulers of the Indian subcontinent prior to British rule in India.*
Qibla	*Direction faced when Muslims pray*
Serangs	*Recruiter and in charge of lascars*
Shahid Minar	*Monument in memory of Bengali language martyrs*
Telwallahs	*Bengali sailors who oiled the engines of a ship*
Zamindar	*Landowner*

Contents

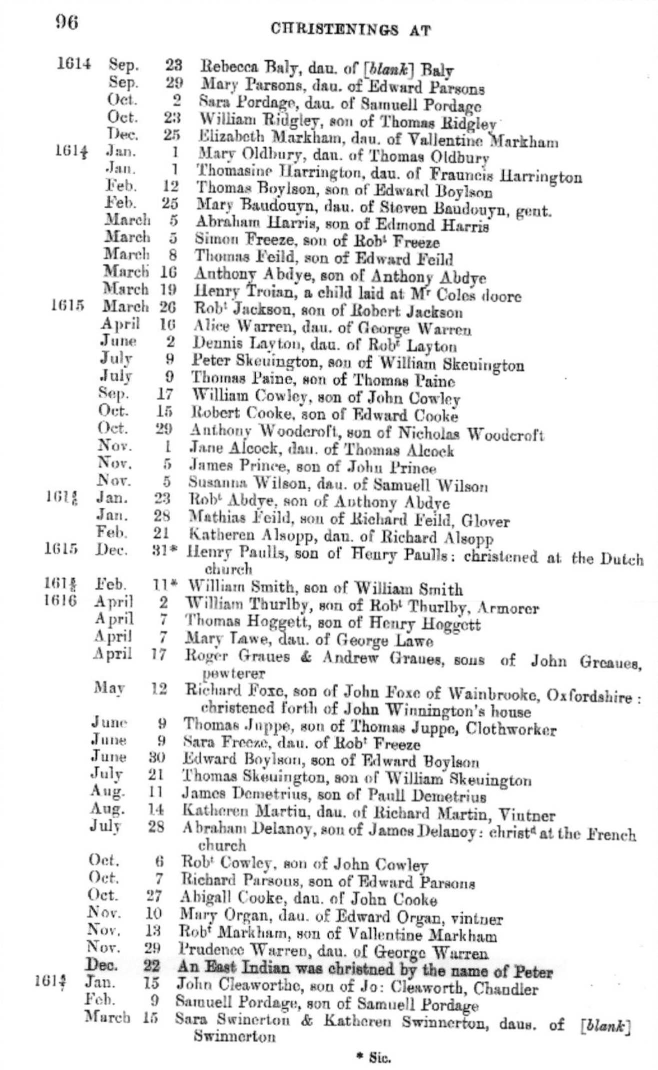

96 CHRISTENINGS AT

1614	Sep.	23	Rebecca Baly, dau. of [*blank*] Baly
	Sep.	29	Mary Parsons, dau. of Edward Parsons
	Oct.	2	Sara Pordage, dau. of Samuell Pordage
	Oct.	23	William Ridgley, son of Thomas Ridgley
	Dec.	25	Elizabeth Markham, dau. of Vallentine Markham
1614/5	Jan.	1	Mary Oldbury, dau. of Thomas Oldbury
	Jan.	1	Thomasine Harrington, dau. of Frauncis Harrington
	Feb.	12	Thomas Boylson, son of Edward Boylson
	Feb.	25	Mary Baudouyn, dau. of Steven Baudouyn, gent.
	March	5	Abraham Harris, son of Edmond Harris
	March	5	Simon Freeze, son of Robt Freeze
	March	8	Thomas Feild, son of Edward Feild
	March	16	Anthony Abdye, son of Anthony Abdye
	March	19	Henry Troian, a child laid at Mr Coles doore
1615	March	26	Robt Jackson, son of Robert Jackson
	April	16	Alice Warren, dau. of George Warren
	June	2	Dennis Layton, dau. of Robt Layton
	July	9	Peter Skeuington, son of William Skeuington
	July	9	Thomas Paine, son of Thomas Paine
	Sep.	17	William Cowley, son of John Cowley
	Oct.	15	Robert Cooke, son of Edward Cooke
	Oct.	29	Anthony Woodcroft, son of Nicholas Woodcroft
	Nov.	1	Jane Alcock, dau. of Thomas Alcock
	Nov.	5	James Prince, son of John Prince
	Nov.	5	Susanna Wilson, dau. of Samuell Wilson
1615/6	Jan.	23	Robt Abdye, son of Anthony Abdye
	Jan.	28	Mathias Feild, son of Richard Feild, Glover
	Feb.	21	Katheren Alsopp, dau. of Richard Alsopp
1615	Dec.	31*	Henry Paulls, son of Henry Paulls: christened at the Dutch church
1615/6	Feb.	11*	William Smith, son of William Smith
1616	April	2	William Thurlby, son of Robt Thurlby, Armorer
	April	7	Thomas Hoggett, son of Henry Hoggett
	April	7	Mary Lawe, dau. of George Lawe
	April	17	Roger Graues & Andrew Graues, sons of John Greaues, pewterer
	May	12	Richard Foxe, son of John Foxe of Wainbrooke, Oxfordshire: christened forth of John Winnington's house
	June	9	Thomas Juppe, son of Thomas Juppe, Clothworker
	June	9	Sara Freeze, dau. of Robt Freeze
	June	30	Edward Boylson, son of Edward Boylson
	July	21	Thomas Skeuington, son of William Skeuington
	Aug.	11	James Demetrius, son of Paull Demetrius
	Aug.	14	Katheren Martin, dau. of Richard Martin, Vintner
	July	28	Abraham Delanoy, son of James Delanoy: christd at the French church
	Oct.	6	Robt Cowley, son of John Cowley
	Oct.	7	Richard Parsons, son of Edward Parsons
	Oct.	27	Abigall Cooke, dau. of John Cooke
	Nov.	10	Mary Organ, dau. of Edward Organ, vintner
	Nov.	13	Robt Markham, son of Vallentine Markham
	Nov.	29	Prudence Warren, dau. of George Warren
	Dec.	**22**	**An East Indian was christned by the name of Peter**
1616/7	Jan.	15	John Cleaworthe, son of Jo: Cleaworth, Chandler
	Feb.	9	Samuell Pordage, son of Samuell Pordage
	March	15	Sara Swinerton & Katheren Swinnerton, daus. of [*blank*] Swinnerton

* Sic.

'Peter', an 'East Indian from the Bay of Bengal', was baptised at St Dionis Church in the City.

Indian units on various fronts during the First World War - Bengal Light Horse on parade. By Permission of the Imperial War Museum Q52664

Introduction

It is commonly believed that the Bengali presence in the UK is something relatively new – from the 1950s, at its earliest, from the years following the Second World War.

In fact, this is very far from the case. The connection goes back over 400 years, right to the beginnings of British involvement in India. [1]

Much of what we know of this history comes from the India Office Records of the Asia Pacific and Africa Collections. These contain the archives of the East India Company (1600-1858), the Board of Control (set up in 1784 to supervise the affairs of the Company), and the India Office (1858-1947). [2]

Books, periodicals and photographic collections add to this wealth of information, as do the personal papers of both British officials and Indian personalities of the time.

India during the Great War 1914-1918: Bengalis for the Front Photograph shows Stretcher drill of Bengal Ambulance Corps, 1917. By Permission of the Imperial War Museum Q110945

The first Bengalis in London

We know that, in 1616, the Mayor of London attended St Dionis Church in the City when 'Peter', an 'East Indian from the Bay of Bengal', was baptised. Peter had arrived in 1614, and his 'Christian' name was chosen by James I.[3] (The 'Bay of Bengal' would refer to today's Bangladesh or West Bengal, India.) Similarly, the archives of St Botolph's Church, next to Aldgate Station, mention that, in 1618, 'James, Indian servant of James Duppa Brewer', a converted Indian Christian (who may have been a Bengali) was buried there.[4]

In 1607, when the East India Company sent its first ships to India, four 'Indians' – possibly Bengalis – already in Britain are identified: 'Marcus', 'John Mendis', 'John Rodrigoe' and 'John Taro'. They are recorded as having sought work on these ships. These men may have arrived from Portugal, as the Portuguese had already established settlements along India's coasts.[5]

British Library sources also mention a Portuguese lascar, 'Manuel De Souza' from Bengal, who died in Erith and was buried ashore in 1760.[6]

Many British men went out to India hoping to make their fortune, and brought young girls home with them on their return, often as 'ayahs' (nannies) to look after the children. Catherine Bengall aged around nine or ten – may have been one such when she came to Britain as a slave of Mr Suthern Davies. She was converted into the Church of England and christened as Catherine Bengall at St James, Westminster, London on 26 Nov 1745. She later had a relationship with a man named William Lloyd, became pregnant and, on 22 Sept 1746 gave birth to a son. He was christened with the father's name, William.[7]

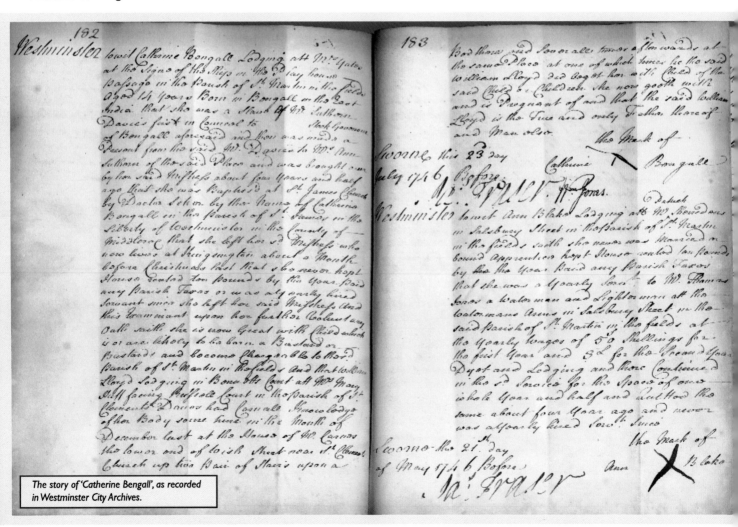

The story of 'Catherine Bengall', as recorded in Westminster City Archives.

The 18th century onwards

The custom of bringing servants 'home' after a spell of duty in India persisted during the 18th century. 'James Turner', born in Calcutta, Bengal, India in about 1754, and recorded as having been baptised in Saint James Church in Islington in 1782, may well have arrived in such a fashion. [8]

We have no way of knowing what the servants themselves thought of being taken from home to a strange city – but it can be imagined. Relationships between employers and employees – who seem often to have been treated as property – clearly broke down at times, as we know from a notice from 1707. This reads:

'Went away from his Master yesterday morning at 4 O'clock, an East Indian Boy, nam'd Caesar, about the age of 16, wearing his own short hair.... He has a handsome face and is tall for his age. Whoever takes him up and brings him to Mr John Waterhouse's, in Aylif Street, Goodman's Fields, shall have ten shillings reward.'[9]

Some other early arrivals in Britain

• Shaikh I'tisam al-Din 1730-1800, born in Nadia, Bengal was appointed by the Mughal Emperor Shah Alam II as a diplomat and given the honorific title 'Mirza'. He arrived in England in 1766 but returned to India three years later. He spoke and wrote about his experiences in Europe in his Persian-language Wonder-book of Europe. Among his observations were lovers flirting in St James Park – like 'peacocks'. [10]

• Raja Rammohon Roy – a Bengali – is often called the 'Maker of Modern India'.
His efforts to protect Hinduism and Indian rights by participating in the British government earned him the title 'The Father of the Bengal Ren-aissance'. He campaigned successfully against the tradition of 'sati' (the burning of a widow on her husband's funeral pyre), making sure that the British ban on this remained in place. He travelled to the UK in 1830 in the course of his campaigning and died in a village near Bristol on 27 September 1833. Rajah Rammohun Roy was the first Indian to involve himself in political activity in Britain. His memorandum submitted to the Parliamentary Committee on Indian Affairs while in England has been described as the first authentic statement of Indian views placed before the British authorities.[11]

• The Bengali poet Michael Madhusadhan Dutt came to London in 1862 to qualify as a barrister. [12]

• Monshee Mahomet Saeed from Bengal, a teacher of Persian and Arabic languages was advertising for pupils in London in 1771. [13]

• In the 1860s Ganendra Mohan Tagore, a professor of Hindu Law and Bengali language taught at University College, London. An Indian prince, the Nawab Nazim of Bengal also arrived in England in 1870, and lived in Edmonton, North London from 1876. [14]

• Shah Abdul Majid Qureshi (Moina Miah) came to London in 1936 as a seaman. In 1938, he opened the Dil Khosh restaurant (destroyed in World War II), and in 1943, with Ayub Ali Master, he formed the Seaman's Welfare League.[15]

• Aftab Ali was the president of All-India Seamen's Federation who made a number of trips to London to represent the interest of Indian seamen. In 1939 he came to London to address a conference on Labour in India. He attended a conference in the name of Indian workers in the UK – 'seamen, unskilled labourers, waiters, peddlers and film extras'. He was also one of the pioneers who had appealed to the UK government to introduce the voucher system whereby employers could bring workers from abroad, and was instrumental in opening a passport office in Sylhet (in his house).[16]

Aftab Ali in 1936.
Image by permission of K R Choudhury.

Aftab Ali, Subhan Chowdhury and H Chowdhury in
London 1954. Image by permission of K R Choudhury.

A Mr and Mrs Rogers set up an ayahs' home and job centre on the corner of India Street in the 1890. Ayahs (nannies) from Bengal, Burma and China could live here while they sought work or a passage home. London Metropolitan University now has a building on the site. [17]

A group of ayahs standing outside the Ayah's Home at no 26 King Edwards's Road, Hackney, 1900.
Credit: Image courtesy of London Borough of Hackney Archives

Women and children fill jugs and cups from the well in Hyde Park, in 1802, while a pet dog drinks from the stream and a picnic table is visible behind them. A uniformed, turbaned servant can be seen in the background. Images like this show the presence of Indian people in London from the 17th century onwards. This man may have been a servant brought to Britain by ex-employees of the East India Company. Like Africans and Caribbeans in similar circumstances, they were more or less treated as slaves.

© Museum of London

Settlements of sailors

Although some early Bengali migrants to Britain were servants, most were sailors recruited in India to work on merchant ships. The majority of Bengali seamen came from Sylhet, and referred to themselves as 'jahajis'.
Their presence was noticed as early as 1765, when an Indian visitor to Britain wrote, 'The English were not unacquainted with [men from] Chatgaon (present day Chittagong) and Juhangeernuggur (Jahangir Nagar – present-day Dhaka).'[18]

Over the years, the community grew slowly, and by the beginning of the 20th century, groups of seamen and ex-soldiers, including a number of Bengalis, had settled near the docks of East End of London, Cable St and the Shadwell area. They joined the small number of Asian professionals – mainly doctors, businessmen and lawyers – who had established themselves in Britain from the middle of the 19th century.

Aftab Ali was the president of All-India Seafarers Federation & Indian Seamen's Union who made a number of trips to London to represent the interest of Indian seamen. In 1933 he represented Indian Labour at International Labour Conference at Geneva. The same year he also attended the Round Table Conference in London as one of the three labour witnesses.

In 1939 he came to London to address a conference on Labour in India. He attended a conference in the name of Indian workers in the UK - 'seamen, unskilled labourers, waiters, peddlers and film extras'. He was also one of the pioneers who had appealed to the UK government to introduce the voucher system whereby employers could bring workers from abroad, and was instrumental in opening a passport office in Sylhet (in his house)
Aftab Ali died in London in 1972 and is buried in Brookwood Cemetery, near Woking.

Today at least 350,000 Bengalis live in Britain.
Most originate from Bangladesh and, often – like the first Bengali settlers – are from the region of Sylhet in the north east of the country. Other Bengalis in the UK come from West Bengal in India. [19]

The first curry in Britain?

In 1778, the East India Company (which, in many ways, operated as a colonial government) appointed a man named Robert Lindsay to collect revenues from local zamindar – landlords in the province of Sylhet (in present-day Bangladesh). Needless to say, this was unpopular, and a riot erupted, during which Lindsay shot a holy man from the local mosque of Shah Jalal.

Unsurprisingly, this made Lindsay exceedingly unpopular, and when he left India he may well have hoped to put the experience behind him. However, he was reminded of it in 1809, when Syed Ullah, the son of one of the holy man's followers, travelled to Britain with a vicar's son returning from India. Syed sought Lindsay out, finding him on a street in the village where he now lived. According to local tradition, the Bengali was invited back to cook what might have been the first curry served to English diners in Britain. (The Bengali sailors, one assumes, had been cooking for each other and on board ship for many years). [20]

Introduction - Footnotes

1 British Library [online]

2 British Library [online]

3 Visram 2002; Jones, 2004; Fisher, 2004 p.27

4 Visram 2002, p.6; Fisher, 2004 p.46

5 Fisher, Michael H; Lahiri, Shompa; Thandi, Shinder, 2007

6 Pereira, C, 2008

7 Fisher, M H, Lahiri, S and Thandi, Shinder, 2007

8 Jones, 2004

9 Tower Hamlets History On-Line [online]

10 Fisher, 2004

11 Visram 1986

12 enotes.com/nineteenth-century-criticism, 2010 [online]

13 Ansari, 2004

14 Visram, 1986

15 Chowdhury, 2001

16 Sherwood, 2007 and Chowdhury, 2001

17 Visram, 2002

18 Visram, 2002, p.15

19 Greater London Authority, 2009 [online]

20 Adams, 1987

Chapter 1

Beginnings

The East India Company

Much immigration, exchange and trade between Britain and the East Indies can trace its roots to the East India Company.

The story of the Company begins during the time of the Mughal Empire of the 1500s and 1600s. Bengal was the richest province, described by the Mughal Emperor Aurangzeb as 'the paradise of nations'. [1]

The availability of good raw materials from Bengal and a highly productive agricultural sector along with a sophisticated division of labour in cloth-production meant that the region soon attracted European merchants. The Portuguese were pioneers, establishing a presence in 1535. A century later, the Dutch took their place, along with the English.

The East India Company was established in 1600 by Royal Charter. Its operations stretched from the Atlantic Ocean to India and South East Asia. [2]

Its ultimate purpose was a profit-making business venture and it eventually led to direct British rule in India. The Company's first trading factory opened in India in 1615. Its ships brought back precious cargoes of goods to east London and, by the 1720s, Bengal was contributing over half of the Company's imports from Asia.

The Company's governors boasted of 'conducting commerce with a sword'. However, its initial attempt to enter the Indian market was prevented by the Mughals. But in 1707, after Aurangzeb had died, the Company used bribery to gain trading rights in Bengal, Hyderabad and Gujarat – before being expelled from Bengal. [3]

Later, the Company – by now dominant in the region, regained its power over Bengal in 1757 at the Battle of Plassey – and its trade between Bengal and Britain began to expand.

Robert Clive and Mir Jafar after the Battle of Plassey, 1757 by Francis Hayman oil on canvas, circa 1760. NPG 5263

Credit: © National Portrait Gallery, London

The Company and the East End

The first East India Company dock had been built as long ago as 1614 near the present day Tower Hamlets Council Town Hall at Mulberry Place, in Blackwall. Over the following centuries, dockyards, warehouses, foundries, saw mills and cordage works grew to meet the needs of the new international shipping industry. This led to a demand for the migration of cheap labour from India. (A parallel growth of factories along the coast of India also created a need for employees to administer this operation – hence the number of British people moving (often temporarily) to India.

The virtual monopoly over Indian trade that the Company held meant that the majority of Indians arriving in Britain in the early 18th century had, one way or another, been employed by the Company. As we have seen, most worked on ships, but house-servants such as ayahs and man-servants working for families returning from India (where they had worked for the Company) added to their number.

Like the seamen, many of the servants would have been Bengali, as Calcutta was one of the East India Company's most important bases. The East India Company's vital importance to the development of the East End and its links to Bengal cannot be overemphasised. [4]

From Company to empire

In the absence of government controls, the Company effectively acted as a ruler of East Asia and India, setting the foundations for Crown rule through the trade of goods and people, the intervention in Indian affairs and ultimately, the establishment of the British Raj in India.

British direct rule over India was established in 1857, and the sub-continent was opened to wider commerce. Indian sailors, who had already been coming to Britain on board East India Company ships, arrived in increasing numbers to work in the British merchant navy or as soldiers maintaining the British Raj in its various overseas colonies.

In 1793, almost £7 million worth of goods were imported into London from 'The East Indies' in heavily militarised ships. The ships usually unloaded downriver and the cargoes were transported to the East India Company warehouses in the City of London in smaller boats and by land. Following the opening of the enclosed West India Docks on the Isle of Dogs in 1802, the valuable East Indies cargoes had become more of a target for river pirates and pilferers who could easily sell teas, silks, saltpetre and spices on the black market.

On 4 August 1806 up to 20,000 people, including members of London's fashionable society, turned out to witness the opening of the East India Docks.

To mark the event, a huge engraved plaque was mounted on the Grand Gate of the Import Dock, through which cotton, silk, tea, spices and porcelain from Bengal, South India, Indonesia and China continued their journey in wagons escorted by the East India Company's own militia westwards to the Company's fortified warehouses in the City of London. The plaque acknowledged the support of the King, Government and East India Company in the building of the docks 'appropriated to the commerce of India' and clearly proclaimed their significance.

The link with the past is visible in the remaining 1806 fortifications, or dock walls, that partially surround the office buildings and are preserved by conservation laws. The road names within the filled-in dock area attempt to reflect the Eastern cargoes, using types of spices such as Nutmeg Lane and Clove Crescent. Modern office buildings relate to river and maritime trades: Lighterman House, Compass House, Anchorage House. The two local Docklands Light Railway stations are called East India and Blackwall. [5]

Lord Clive (1725-1774) receiving from the Nawab of Bengal the grant of the sum of money which was applied to establish the fund for disabled officers and soldiers known as Lord Clive's Fund. Originally published/produced in 1772-1773. Illustrator: Penny, Edward (1714-1791) Photo credit: Lord Clive & Nawab of Bengal © The British Library Board Shelfmark/Page: Foster 91,

Lascars

The East India Company recruited large numbers of seamen, who (as we saw in the Introduction) formed the first sizable South Asian community in Britain. They included Bengalis, who settled in London's East End. Many took up jobs on the merchant ships, which carried goods between Assam, Bengal and beyond.

These early Bengali seamen were commonly referred to as 'lascars'. The word was once used to describe any sailor from the Indian sub-continent or any other part of Asia, but came particularly to refer to people from West Bengal and modern-day Bangladesh.

It comes from the Persian Lashkar, meaning 'military camp', and 'al-askar', the Omani word for a guard or soldier.

Lascars were employed on European ships from the 17th century to the start of the 20th century. The East India Company was not the only employer – the establishment of the Indian Terminus of the P&O shipping company in Calcutta in 1842 also led to the employment of large numbers of Bengali Lascars. In all cases, they tended to be at the bottom of British Merchant Navy hierarchies and were often denied employment rights.[6]

25th February 1942: Indian merchant seamen played an important role in World War II.
Here, two seamen, Ismail Mahomed Xyequb and Ana Mian, are pictured having received British Empire Medals.

An Indian 'lascar' seaman at King George V Dock, 1959 © Museum of London

Indian seamen in 1942, on shore leave pass the time by playing cards. Seamen such as these played a vital role in the war effort.

(Photo by Al Fenn/Pix Inc./Time Life Pictures/Getty Images, credit Time Life/getty Images)

The Sylhet connection

The majority of the Asian seamen from Bengal came from one district – Sylhet, the north-eastern area of modern day Bangladesh. As sailing ships ceased to be used, and steamships took their place, men from Sylhet mostly worked in the engine rooms. Seamen from Noakhali worked on the decks, while numbers of other sailors came from Chittagong.

Sylhet had fallen under British rule in 1765. In the mid-19th century, when the British introduced steam-driven ships travelling between Assam and Calcutta, carrying tea and other goods. They recruited boatmen of Sylhet, mainly as engine room crews. This was the first historical step towards the custom of employing men from Sylhet as steamer crews. The first shipping companies to employ Bengali crews were The Clan and the Orient Line. [7]

Some Sylhetis were known as 'donkeywallahs' (because the engines were 'donkey engines') and those who greased and oiled machinery were known as 'telwallahs'. Others worked supplying the furnace with coal and disposing of the ashes. The working conditions were harsh and hot, and many seamen died of heat stroke and exhaustion.

Many cooks employed by the Royal Navy also came from Sylhet, and there are records of Sylhetis working in London restaurants as early as 1873. Arriving in the London Docks, lascars would try to find fellow-Asians with whom to stay, thus beginning a tradition of migration from the Sylhet, Chittagong and Comilla regions that continued over the centuries. [8]

A Map of the Eastern Parts of Hindoostan; Containing the Soubabs or Kingdoms of Bengal, Bahar, Awd, and Ellahabad. Drawn chiefly from actual Surveys; 1769 Engraved by William Whitchurch 1776. © Royal Geographical Society (with IBG)

Maps dating from the 19th century indicate the areas of Bengal where the lascars mainly came from – and which are the ancestral homes of many Bengalis in Britain today.

No one is quite sure why so many seamen came from Sylhet. Speculation among the Bengali seamen themselves is that it was because the serangs (Recruiter and in charge of lascars) who operated in the streets of Calcutta chose to recruit crews from their own birthplace – that is, Sylhet. Crews were also recruited in Calcutta to carry Assamese tea, including tea from Sylhet. Some seamen suggested other reasons. For example, Haji Kona Miah, a seaman interviewed by Caroline Adams in her book, Across Seven Seas and Thirteen Rivers, said: 'The Sylhet people were in the ship because these people follow each other, and some went there and others saw them, and they thought they could get jobs too. It all started before we were born.' [9]

Yousuf Choudhury, a seaman himself, gives another reason: 'In the distant past, the … province of Assam had only water-way communications with the rest of India. Sylhet was a district of Assam … with low land in its middle part, connected with Bengal in the west. The short cut waterways from central Assam were through Sylhet. Sylhet set a tradition of mercantile boats in the lowland and was started by the early settlers.' [10]

The British discovered the mountains of Assam were an ideal place for growing tea. Steamships were by now in use, and these could sail right up the Kushiara River, in Sylhet, to collect the tea. Those ships also needed stokers, and adventurous young men from villages along the Kushiara River jumped at the new opportunities on board ship.

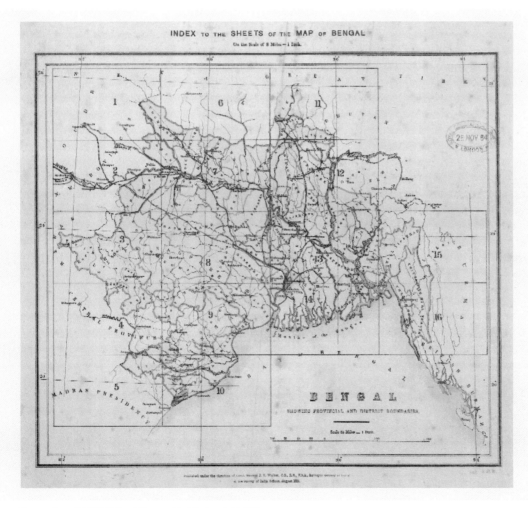

Eastern Bengal 1903 © Royal Geographical Society (with IBG)

The living conditions of Bengali seamen

Throughout the 18th and 19th centuries, lascars lives were often poverty-stricken and hard. Abused by their employers on board, they were left to their own devices once their ships had docked. Outright cruelty led many to feel they had no choice but to jump ship. Joseph Salter, a 'Missionary to the Orientals and Africans' working in the mid-19th century, tells how the entire lascar crew of Muslims deserted after the ship docked in the Thames because while on board they had been forced to eat pork, flogged and hung up with weights tied to their feet – wounding some of them fatally. Their bodies had been thrown overboard. [11]

Others were just abandoned without wages in London by unscrupulous employers. This was partly a result of the 1660 Navigation Act (repealed in 1849), which stipulated that crews on ships importing goods and returning to Asia had to be three-quarters English. As a result, if a the ship arrived in Britain with a crew made up of more than 25 per cent of Asians, some would inevitably be forced out of employment, and become stranded in London. [12]

In 1782, East India Company records describe lascars arriving at their Leadenhall Street offices 'reduced to great distress and applying to us for relief'. In 1785 a letter writer in the Public Advertiser wrote of 'miserable objects, lascars, that I see shivering and starving in the streets.' [13]

Many lascars died in the streets of East End, especially in winter. It was estimated that before 1810, 130 lascars died in Britain each year (making 2,600 in 20 years). During the severe winter of 1813, nine deaths occurred on one single day. [14]

In 1814, a Parliamentary Committee of Inquiry that made a surprise visit to some barracks where lascars were staying:
… found the rooms to be dirty, with no bedding or furniture, the lascars slept on the floors. There were no fireplaces and the men were only given one blanket each. The sick had neither separate quarters nor a hospital.' [15]

In the following years, the plight of the lascars continued to raise concerns in various quarters. In 1842, a letter published in the Sailors Magazine read, 'Last winter … hundreds of them were … left to sleep in the open air … with scarcely an article of clothing; while in every part of the city they might be seen engaged in sweeping the … streets for a chance pence.' [16]

Those seamen who lost their ships or were left stranded even resorted to begging. Sailors, whether passing through or stranded, tended to rely on riverside lodging places, before returning home. From 1795, lascar hostels and seamen's homes were set up in Shoreditch, Shadwell and Wapping. Residents intended that these should be temporary bases rather than the start of a permanent community (though this was not always an option).

Even in such places, seamen suffered from gross neglect. Often, they lived in appalling conditions, unfit for human habitation, and were herded like cattle, six to eight people in a single room without any furniture or bedding. The death toll was high: in one estimation, at least 10 per cent of all seamen who arrived in England died. In 1854, the coroner of East Middlesex felt so strongly about the plight of lascars that he wrote to Lord Palmerston, the Home Secretary.

Census return for the Strangers Home Residents 1861 Census.

Charitable organisations

For a time, it was left to charitable organisations to do what they could for stranded sailors. As early as 1786 a 'Committee of Gentlemen' had been set up to organise relief for the distressed lascars. The Committee changed its name to 'Committee for the Relief of the Black Poor' to provide relief and prevent recurring distress in the future including plans for resettlement in Sierra Leone. In 1787 around 350 people were selected to be sent to Sierra Leone, 'one was a 29 year old Bengal born lascar, John Lemon. He was a hairdresser and a cook, and had arrived in Britain on a naval ship.' [17] (Lemon married an Englishwoman named Elizabeth. Records show they survived the voyage to Africa, but nothing was heard of them after that.) [18]

More than 60 years later, in the winter of 1850, 'some 40 sons of India' were found dead of cold and hunger on the streets of London. In response to such tragedies, a Society for the Protection of Asian Sailors was formed in 1857. It founded the Stranger's Home in Limehouse, in East India Dock Road, to meet the needs of destitute sailors. [19]

Even many Christian missionaries, who might have been expected to show concern, considered the seamen to be ignorant and wicked: the Hindus, they felt, worshipped idols, while the Muslims followed a false prophet. Neither were thought fit for normal housing.

However, in 1856, various Christian missionary societies took the initiative to set up the foundation for 'The Strangers Home for seaman from Asia, Africa and South Sea Islands'. In 1857, The Strangers Home in West India Road was officially opened. A block of flats called West India House stands today on the original site of The Strangers Home, next to Limehouse Police Station. [20]

The 'Strangers Home', shown here as it appeared in the mid-1930s, was set up for sailors from south Asia and elsewhere. Today, the site is occupied by a block of flats.

Strangers Home, 1937 © Tower Hamlets Local History Library and Archives

Relationships with local people

There are few records of any positive relationship between local people and the Bengali seamen. The locals saw the seamen as dirty (which, given their living conditions, was hardly their fault) and tended to blame them for their poor health, and some records demonstrate that they tried to steal from them. For example, in 1764, John Ryan and his wife, Mary, were convicted of theft from John Morgan, who was formerly called Abdullah. In court, Morgan said:

> 'I was born at Bengal. I have come here twice before, with Indiamen; and have been in England this time about seven months. I came over with a tyger for Sir George Pigot, who was governor of Madrass, and attend upon it for him now. I went from his house in Soho-square, where I live, to see a friend near Rosemary-lane, about four months ago, and staying later than ordinary, I wanted a lodging: I was recommended to the house of the prisoner, which I believe to be a bawdy-house.' [21]

In a letter dated 28 November 1809, Hilton Docker, a medical doctor to the lascars described their conditions:

> 'The Natives of India who come to this country are mostly of bad constitutions. Numbers are landed sick from the ships, where they have been ill, and when they arrive (usually at the latter end of the year) they have to encounter with a climate and season to them particularly pernicious which most frequently increase their disease. Those who are landed in health are of course exposed to the same danger of climate and season and in addition almost all of them give way to every excess in drinking and debauchery, and contract to a violent degree those diseases (particularly venereal) which such habits are calculated to produce.' [22]

Given the way poverty and prejudice limited the opportunities for socialising, none of this should be very surprising. Like sailors everywhere, stranded lascars seeking entertainment often frequented pubs, gambling houses and prostitutes. For example, Indian Lascars were involved in an affray involving Chinese sailors in Stepney in 1785. [23]

Asian seamen also got into conflict with the locals: '… in 1803, three lascars armed with cutlasses broke into the City of Carlisle public house in Shoreditch High Street, seeking to recover the substantial sum of £150 they claimed that local sex workers there had stolen from them.' [24]

In 1852, Elizabeth Allen and Mahomet Abraham lived near the corner of what are now Chicksand/Spelman Streets – but was then known as Little Halifax Street. The authorities and Elizabeth's family decided that she must be mad or bad to live with a blind lascar:

> Mahomet Abraham, a native of Calcutta, East Indies. He was brought to this country in the barque Diana, Captain Brown [in 1844]; was kept ashore in the Infirmary, Liverpool, for fever and inflammation in the eyes, where he was deprived of his precious sight. Being a stranger, far, far away from home, he is forced to trust to the kind, benevolent, and humane, who feel for the misfortunes of others.

> Earlier exertions were successfully made to get her cured of a complication of loathsome disorders at Bartholomew's Hospital, from whence, after being brought to a state of convalescence, and robbing some of the nurses of small sums of money.

> 'After the Mendicity case he was put in a poor house and she was forced by her parents to emigrate.' [25]

Tensions with other communities

There were occasionally fights amongst the lascars themselves, as well as seamen from other nationalities both within barracks where they lived and outdoors (as in the case of the Indian and Chinese sailors 1785 discussed above).

This was partly because other communities felt threatened by Asian seamen taking their jobs especially at a time of economic hardship: 'Irish lumpers [labourers] fought street battles against Chinese seamen unloading their ships in July 1813 and against Indian lascars in August.' [26]

It was said that the Chinese usually fought over gambling and the Indians after a having a drink. In 1806, 150 Indians fought 300 Chinese who were supported by Arab seamen. In another incident 1803, one Friday night, lascars seized the streets near Tower of London, claiming that one of their lascar comrades had been robbed by a sex worker. This took place in Rosemary Lane, now called Royal Mint Street . [27]

Local dockers responded to events like this by making a point of liaising with Serangs, in an attempt to gain control over the lascars. Even as recently as the 1980s, a dockers trade union official referred to Bengali community leaders as 'serangs'. [28]

Send them home!

By the beginning of the Napoleonic Wars (1803-15), over a thousand lascars had arrived in the Port of London. Most arrived on East India Company ships (though, later, they later on came on P&O and Clan Line vessels). [30]

Despite the fact that the East India Company had, in most cases, brought the seamen to London, it was reluctant to take the responsibility for them. The government intervened in with initiatives to return the lascars to India, passing the Merchant Shipping Amendment Act in 1855. This meant the Company was obliged to take responsibility for this.

In 1871 Board of Trade appointed transfer officers with the purpose of sending back Asian seamen via India-bound ships. In 1894 another law was enacted to ensure lascars returned to India. Officers who engaged in crackdowns on lascars in Britain claimed to be motivated by humanitarian aims: they hoped to prevent potential deserters from wandering into lives of destitution on the streets of Britain. [31]

Riots at the warehouses

The influx of foreign sailors was far from being the only – or even main – cause of tension that resulted from the growth of trade with India. Cheap imports were also a source of unrest. Today, the East India Company's Cutler Street warehouses are used as office blocks, while the site of another tea warehouse, Potters Field, is the home of the Greater London Authority. The warehouses once held a vast range of exotic products such as spices, indigo and ivory, as well as opium, grown in Bengal and sold in China to finance the tea trade. But the real cause for concern was the importation of cheap cloth – including calico cotton and silks – also from Bengal. In 1699, angry local weavers, protesting at this, stormed East India House.

The following year, the importation of dyed and printed cottons from the East was banned in Britain, causing devastation in Bengal. [29]

The Merchant Shipping Act

In 1894, the Merchant Shipping Act reiterated the fact that lascar contracts bound them to return to India. Its infamous section 125 gave ship owners enhanced powers to place lascars in crews heading back to India.

Section XXIII of the Merchant Shipping Act Amendment Act, 1855 states:

> When a lascar or Indian native seaman is engaged in India to serve as a seaman in a voyage from India to the United Kingdom and back to India, and when for any reason such lascar is transferred from the ship in which he proceeded from India to any other ship in any port or ports of the United Kingdom bound to any port in India, a further agreement must be entered into between the master of the ship to which he is transferred and the lascar or seaman. [32]

In fact, few shipping companies made warrants against the lascar deserters. Some ex-seamen felt free to apply to the High Commissioner for India to obtain Certificates of Nationality and the British Indian Seamen's Certificates of Identity: these documents are to all intents and purposes passports, and were regarded as such by their holders.

In 1937, there were only two shipping companies – the P&O and the Ellerman Lines which took out warrants concerning Indian seamen deserting their ships. The offenders were often arrested or became the subject of police inquiry.

It is worth noting that the lascars endured hostility from British trade unions, notably the National Union of Seamen under Havelock Wilson and a range of politicians including Clement Attlee who, speaking in Parliament in 1932, asked 'Why do we not have English sailors in English ships?' [33]

Twentieth century

Despite the various initiatives and attempts to send back the lascars, with time a small community of them grew, especially in the East End of London. Some of the seamen set up their own lodging houses. During the First World War more lascars were needed as local crews were engaged with the British navy. As a result the numbers of Asian lascars grew further. [34] By the end of the First World War Indian seafarers made up 20 per cent of the British maritime labour force. [35]

East India House, Leadenhall Street, 1829
© Museum of London

This picture shows the exterior of East India House, the headquarters of the East India Company, in around 1829. East India House was demolished 1862 to make way for the Royal Mail Steamship Lines, and later, the Lloyds building.

The changing face of the East India Docks

These four pictures show how the East India Docks has changed over the last 200 years: the first shows the dock as it was in 1808, when it was the hub of East India Company's activities. The second shows the grand entrance to the dock, just over 100 years later, in 1912. Seafaring was still of major importance in the area and the ships, which were relatively small, still made use of the dock.

But by 1971 – shown in the third picture – the area was all but derelict, following bombing in the Second World War and the migration of business to modern container ports. Today, (see the fourth picture) the area has become the site of prestige office blocks and expensive water-front housing.

East India Docks, 1808 © Tower Hamlets Local History Library and Archives

*Entrance to East India Dock, 1912
© Tower Hamlets Local History
Library and Archives*

East India Docks from All Saints Church, Poplar, 1971 © Tower Hamlets Local History Library and Archives

East India Dock basin, 2010 © Kois Miah/Swadhinata Trust

St Matthias Church (113 High Street, Poplar)

Poplar Chapel, 1799
© Tower Hamlets
Local History Library
and Archives

The story goes that the East India Company bought land in Poplar in 1627, using a bequest from a diamond merchant it had employed, but who had made a fortune from embezzling precious stones. The company used the land, which was close to its own dockyard, for almshouses. In 1564, it built the church – which later became St Matthias Church – as an accompanying chapel, known as 'Poplar Chapel'. The first picture shows the chapel in 1799, having been reconstructed in 1776. In 1866 the building passed to the Ecclesiastical Commissioners and the following year the Parish of St Matthias came into being (seen in the second picture).

The church is one of the few physical remains of the East India Company. Old masts of ships, said to be from the masts of East Indiamen, were used as arch supports for the entire building, while the Company's coat of arms is carved on the ceiling inside the church. Tombstones of East India Company managers are set into its floors. The third picture, shows the interior of the church.

St Matthias survived the 'blitz' of the Second World War, which brought devastation to much of the rest of Docklands, relatively unscathed, but was eventually closed in the mid-1970s. However, it was recognised as an important historical building (the oldest in Docklands) and as such, was restored in the 1990s – but not as a place of worship.

The bright and broad interior of the original Puritan chapel has returned to its original state. The building now serves as a community centre.

As such, it is mainly used by people of Bengali origin whose presence in London can, like the building itself, be traced back to the activities of the East India Company. [36]

St Matthias Community Centre, 2010
© Swadhinata Trust Photo Ansar Ahmed Ullah

Interior of St Matthias Community Centre showing pillars made of old ship masts, 2010
© Swadhinata Trust Photo Ansar Ahmed Ullah

The East Indiaman, the Duchess of Athol undergoing refurbishment in
1821 in Blackwall Yard. This picture shows commerce in the area at
the height of the East India Company's power.

© Tower Hamlets Local History Library and Archives, Duchess of Atholl

Settlers in the 1950s

Among the settlers who arrived in the East End in the 1950s was Syed Abdul Kadir, who now lives in Poplar. He served in the Pakistan Navy from 1950 before retiring as a marine engineer in 1972. He came to the UK in 1953 to attend the Queen's Coronation at Westminster Abbey as guard of honour of Pakistan Naval ship, PNS Zulfiquar. During Pakistan's war with India in 1965 he was in active service.

During Bangladesh Liberation War in 1971 he escaped West Pakistan to fight with Bengali freedom fighters.

Syed Abdul Kadir in the Navy, 1979

Sea Captain Shiv Banerjee came to the UK in 1967, arriving at Tilbury Docks, as a cadet with the India Steamship Company. He then sailed around different parts of the world as an Officer in the Merchant Navy. In 1975 he studied at the School of Navigation which is now the London Metropolitan University site at Tower Gateway. The pictures also show his Master's Certificate and Seaman's Identity Card –part of which is in Bengali. In the early days he lived at Beacon House, Dock Street – then, a seaman's hostel.

Unemployed sailors registered at an office in Prescot street that later became a DHSS centre. He is married and at present lives with his wife at Toynbee Hall.

Photo taken in 1977 on way to Shanghai China © Captain Shiv Banerjee

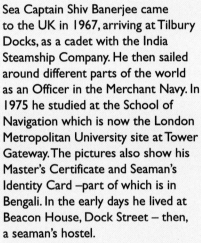

1 December 1928: Lascars at the Opening of the Tower Hill Memorial. (Photo by Fox Photos/Getty Images)

The Tower Hill Memorial was opened on 1 December, 1928. At the time, it commemorated those merchant seamen lost during the First World War and for whom there was no known grave. An extension bears the names of similar losses during the Second World War.

The tradition of Bengalis serving as merchant seamen continues, with about 8,000 working in international shipping companies. At the same time, Bangladesh's second largest city, Chittagong, has been the world's primary site for the dismantling of large ships. Through the course of time, a shipbuilding industry has also developed in Bangladesh.

Tower Hill Memorial

A monument commemorating British Merchant Seamen who lost their lives in the First and Second World Wars can be seen in Trinity Square Gardens, near Tower Hill tube station.

Many of the names on the monument indicate seamen of Bengali origin – such as Miah, Latif, Ali, Choudhury or Uddin – stokers, greasers, coal trimmers and firemen from the engine rooms, and cooks from the galleys. However, these named individuals only represent the privileged few Bengalis employed as British crew members, and exclude some 4-5000 lascars who died at sea and whose names were never known. [37]

Indian sources give the figure of 3,427 lascars dead and 1,200 taken prisoners in the First World War. They also give an estimate of 6,600 Indian seamen dead, 1,022 wounded and 1,217 taken prisoner in the Second World War.[38] Employed at a fraction of the normal rate for seamen, lascars trapped in the engine rooms suffered a particularly high casualty rate.

Official tables exclude lascars amongst the names of 26,833 killed, despite the fact that they made up 50,000 of 190,000 crew members at war.[39]

2010 © Swadhinata Trust, Photo Ansar Ahmed Ullah

Chapter 1 - Footnotes

1 Robins, 2006

2 Robins, 2006

3 Robins 2006

4 Robins, 2006

5 Wemyss, 2008, p.57

6 Wemyss, 2009

7 Choudhury, 1993

8 Change Institute, 2009

9 Adams, 1994, p.28

10 Choudhury, 1993, p.29

11 Visram 1986

12 Wemyss 2009

13 Public Advertiser, 1785

14 Visram, 1986, p.40

15 Visram 1986, p.44

16 Visram 1986, p.48

17 Fryer, 1984, pp.94–202

18 Robins, 2006

19 Jones, 2004

20 Visram, 1986 p.49

21 Old Bailey [online], 2010

22 British Library: Help for researchers [online]

23 Fisher, 2006

24 Fisher, 2006 p.160

25 Fisher, 2006, p.387

26 Fisher, 2006 p.163

27 Fisher, 2006

28 Greater London Trade Union Resource Unit, 1985

29 Jones, 2004

30 The Ships' List, 2007 [online]

31 Moving Here, Tracing your Roots [online]

32 Merchant Shipping Act Amendment Act, Section XXIII (quoted in Moving Here, Tracing your roots [online])

33 Sherwood, p. 199

34 Visram, 1986

35 Wemyss, 2009

36 St Matthias Community Centre, 2009 [online]

37 Jones, 2004 and Commonwealth War Graves Commission [website]

38 Our Merchant Seamen, 1947

39 Adams, 1987; Visram, 2002

Chapter 2

A roof over their heads

Settlement and the first Bengali communities

Even during the early 19th century worries had been expressed about the condition of lascar seamen's living quarters, and there was some attempt to acknowledge the need to regulate them.

A Parliamentary Committee in 1814-15 on lascars and other Asiatic Seamen reported that: 'A small number only was in the barracks at the time which Your Committee visited them, but they understood that there were periods of the year, when no less than 1,000 or 1,100 persons were received into them; a number which Your Committee observe, exceeds the utmost calculation of the number for which they are intended, or for which they can afford reasonable accommodation, consistently with a due regard to the comfort, health and cleanliness of the people, which latter, even in their present uncrowded state of the barracks, there was a great deficiency, owing probably in a great degree to the habits of the Lascars themselves.'[1]

A group of 'lascars' in the early 19th century, among whom are Bengali, Malay, Siamese, Burmese, Chinese and Surati seamen.

© British Library Board

LASCARS.

BURMESE   BENGALI   MALAY   SIAMESE   SURATI

CHINESE

The East End is full of places where once lascars made their home for longer or shorter periods while they were ashore in London. Barracks – very basic accommodation – existed in Shoreditch, Shadwell and St Georges's in the East. Lascar missions were operated by St Luke's Church in Canning Town and the London City Mission (whose accommodation was called the Lascar Institute). Lodgings could also be found in Kingsland Road, Shoreditch, Hackney Road and Shadwell, as well as in the 'Passmore Edwards Sailors' Palace', run by the British and Foreign Sailors Society, West India Dock Road. This was built in 1901 for the British and Foreign Sailors' Society and is now owned by a housing association. Perhaps most famously, there was Society for the Protection of Asian Sailors 'Strangers' Home' in West India Dock Road (see page 23).

In 1924, The Mission – also known as the Empire Memorial Hostel – opened on Commercial Road opened. It is now luxury apartments. In fact, only one maritime charity remains in operation today: Queen Victoria Seamen's Rest in Commercial Road. This Art Nouveau neo-Tudor building was opened in 1902, starting life in 1843 in the Methodist Chapel in Cable Street, later moving to the present site. As it has always done, this part of the East End provides accommodation and support to seafarers from all over the world.[2]

At this time, the Bengali community remained relatively small and mostly transient – and more likely to accept living for short periods in 'barracks' or extremely overcrowded hostels. Things changed dramatically during the 20th century.

Firstly, even in the early years of the century, while it was still the case that most seamen returned to their ships after a short stay, the experience of that stay was becoming something of interest to governments of the time. Putting aside the humanitarian aspect of the issue, the growing clamour for independence in India, made the issue particularly sensitive.

This is shown by the records of the Economic Department, covering the period of the 1920s and 1930s, which dealt with questions relating to Asians in Britain and concerns about lascar accommodation in Britain in the 1920s.[3] Inspectors and Health Officers condemned as 'quite unsuitable' the cheaper common lodging-houses in St George Street, Stepney, used by some British Ship-ping Companies, and the 'godown' used by the P&O as 'an abomination'.[4]

A report of a Conference held at the India Office held on 22 February, 1923 reported:

Our position is, if – which I hope will not occur – any scandal should arise in regard to the position of Indian seamen in this country, if, for example, in a common lodging-house there was a fracas in which Indian and British seamen might be injured, public opinion in India, which is rather critical in all these matters, will not unnaturally say – 'what has the Secretary of State for India been doing to look after the interests of these fellow countrymen of ours who are in this country?' It is a bad thing that these Indian seamen are mixed up with other races including British seamen. Certain touts managed to get hold of these men.[5]

As an alternative, they recommended housing lascars in the Asiatic Home – formerly known as the Strangers Home – see page 23 (Chapter 1). Other, similar establishments were gradually being set up –. One was located in what is now Wilton's Music Hall, Grace's Alley, Ensign Street. The Methodist East End Mission took it over in 1888 and the mahogany bar was converted into a coffee house for around 1,000 people. It had beds for 30 people and there were always black sailors seeking accommodation there.[6]

Secondly, the South Asian community was beginning to change noticeably – and with it, the type of housing it needed. After the First World War, in the 1920s and then, increasingly, in the mid-1930s, the number of seamen jumping ship and looking for longer-term accommodation – steadily grew. A community was beginning to put down roots.

Seaman Sona Miah described how he came to London: 'Coming Glasgow, 1937, I run away from ship to London. Other people telling, 'London very good'. That time, England very good, people were respect coloured people. Coming to house near New Road – I take address when come to London before.'[7]

Sona Miah's experience in London shows that there was now the beginning of a community that was able to give support and help to its own members. A few important individuals stand out.

Mr Munshi and his hostel

Mr Munshi arrived in London in 1922. He settled at first at 16 Elder Street (now demolished), and the name of Elder Street is mentioned by other seamen at this time. Mr Munshi later ran a lodging house in Code Street, off Brick Lane, for Bengali seamen. (Things don't change much: this street is now the site of a hostel for homeless people.) It proved a haven for newly-arrived Bengalis.

Seaman Shah Abdul Majid Qureshi describes his arrival:

'I had one or two addresses, but they were wrongly written … and when I showed them to anyone, they didn't know what to do … cannot go back to my ship … I suddenly saw a young man, about 25, very dark looking … I thought, probably he is from Madras … he spoke to me in Sylhet dialect … I was very glad, I held him, embraced him … He said, "You come from the boat?" I said, "Yes". He said, "Come with me, I will give shelter, I live in Mr Munshi's house."'[8]

Ayub Ali Master

Another early and influential Bengali figure connected to this area was Ayub Ali Master. He ran a seamen's café in Commercial Road in the 1920s and also then opened the Shah Jalal Coffee House at 76, Commercial Street, now Dino's Grill. Ayub Ali Master turned his home into a vital centre of support for Bengalis which included a lodging house, job centre offering letter writing and form filling, an education service, travel agency and advice bureau. He started the Indian Seamen's Welfare League in 1943 and, subsequently, (between 1945-59) went to live at 13, Sandy's Row. [9]

2010 © Swadhinata Trust, Photo Lovely Khanom

*Ayub Ali Master:
Source page 69, Choudhury,
Yousuf 'The Roots and Tales
of Bangladeshi Settlers',
Sylheti Social History Group,
1993 by kind permission of
Sherwan Chowdhury*

*Ayub Ali Master in the
middle with nephews Somuj
Miah on right and Mofazzul
Hussain, London 1950
Image: Courtesy Ragged
School Museum*

New accommodation has also been built with Bengali names including:

• The Shahjalal Estate, (named after the Sufi Saint of Sylhet and owned by the Spitalfields Housing Association, which was formed in 1979. This is on Fakhruddin Street (formerly Peace Street), itself named after a community activist and the founder of Spitalfields Housing Association.

• The Plassey Buildings (2003), Dod Street, Poplar, named after the historic battle of Plassey.

• Burhanuddin House. E1 - 1989, (old Police Station), Commercial Street, named after a saint of Sylhet, Sheikh Burhan Uddin.

• Zafar Khan House (old Field House), Hanbury Street, E1. Rehabilitated tenement block , completed in 1988 and named after the late community worker Zafar Khan.

• Surma Close, (named after the main river that flows through Sylhet) Selby Street, off Vallance Road. Newly developed family housing, built in 1988-89.

• Mannan Buildings, Roman Road. Newly built flats named after a former tenant board member of Spitalfields Housing Association who died in 2009.

• Aftab Ali Terrace (the campaigner described above who fought for the rights of seamen and persuaded the British government to support their rehabilitation in the UK. He was Secretary of the Indian Seamen Union, International delegate to the ILO, and Member of Pakistan Parliament (MNA) from Balagonj, Biswanath. The terrace is in a housing development built in in 1995 in Tent Street, off Brady Street, E1.

Shahjalal Estate, Fakhruddin Street (Old Peace Street): Vallance Road. 2010 © Kois Miah/Swadhinata Trust

Zafar Khan House (Old Field House), Hanbury Street. 2010 © Kois Miah/Swadhinata Trust

Surma Close in Selby Street, off Vallance. 2010 © Kois Miah/Swadhinata Trust

Plassey Building, Dod Street. 2010 © Kois Miah/ Swadhinata Trust

Aftab Terrace, Tent Street. 2010 © Kois Miah/Swadhinata Trust

Mitali Housing Association was set up in 1985 by a pioneering group of Bengalis that included Alhaj Shofique Miah, Chunu Miah, Tuta Miah and Enayeth Sarwar to provide homes for members of their community. Mitali Housing has around four hundred properties and has named Miah Terrace and Mitali (meaning friendship) Passage in Whitechapel. Miah Terrace is named after Mitali's various founding members who shared the name Miah.

Chapter 2 - Footnotes

1 British Library: Help for Researchers: Asians in Britain: Ayahs, Servants and Sailors Marine Department Records [online])

2 Tower Hamlets Council [online]

3 British Library, Help for researchers: Asians in Britain: Ayahs, Servants and Sailors: Records of the Economic Department [online]

4 British Library, Help for researchers: Asians in Britain: Ayahs, Servants and Sailors: Records of the Economic Department [online]

5 British Library, Help for researchers: Asians in Britain: Ayahs, Servants and Sailors: Records of the Economic Department [online]

6 London Borough of Tower Hamlets (Black History Walks)

7 Adams, 1994 p.41

8 Adams, 1994, p.41

9 Jones, 2004

Chapter 3

Dyes and textiles

A long tradition

From 17th century weaving in Fournier Street to 20th century textile workshops in Commercial Road, the East End has made a name for itself as the centre of London's textile industries.

The story of the East London clothing industry has four main chapters. It began with the Protestants feeling persecution in continental Europe - initially 'Flemish and Walloon' in the sixteenth century and later the French Huguenots –who had brought their skills in silk-weaving. They made Spitalfields silk a world-famous product in the 17th and 18th centuries. From the late 17th century the East India Company began importing fabrics from India which competed with the Spitalfields fabrics.

The painted cotton textiles that were imported from India during the 17th and 18th centuries transformed dress and furnishings in Britain. Cotton was practically unknown in England before these Indian textiles appeared – ordinary people wore linen and woollen garments, while the rich also favoured French and Italian silks. The brilliantly coloured, light, washable cottons took Britain (as well as Holland and France) by storm, and by the 18th century 'chintz' was the fabric of choice for dress and furnishing throughout the country. Other highly prized textiles from India included the diaphanous muslins of Bengal and beautifully soft Kashmir shawls, both of which were eminently suitable for the neo-classical styles of dress that were fashionable during the late 18th and early 19th centuries.[1]

The author Daniel Defoe was one of those who protested at the new fashions – the Calico Madams and the women who had promoted 'the chintz from… their floors to their backs'.[2]

The Weaver's complaint against the Callico [sic] Madams, 1719
The cost little pay
And are tawdery gay
…
To neglect their own Works
Employ pagans and Turks
And let foreign Trump'ry o'er spread them
…
They're so Callico wise
Their own growth they despise
And without an inquiry, 'Who made 'em'[3]

The Spitalfields weavers protested against these imports. In January 1697, 5,000 weavers marched on Parliament. In March they attacked the home of Thomas Bohun the Deputy Governor of the East India Company who lived in Spitalfields.[4]

In 1720 rioters threatened to demolish James Dalbiac's House at 20 Spital Square after the House of Lords rejected a bill to ban calicos.[5]

In the first half of the 18th century the Indian weavers were relatively well-paid but after the battle of Plassey in 1757, conditions deteriorated rapidly for them.[6]

Indigo was India's major dyestuff until the mid-20th century, widely used both locally and for export. Although it was already being traded as a luxury to Europe the expanding spice trade carried on the East Indiamen (ships) led to increasing quantities of indigo dyestuff and dyed textiles being available in the markets of London and Amsterdam. The ramifications of indigo production in Bengal caused the 'Blue Mutiny' of 1859, and even influenced India's Independence movement.[7]

From the late 19th to the mid-20th century Jewish tailors dominated the industry as many Jewish people came from Eastern Europe escaping persecution and found work in their new home. In the second half of the 20th century Bengalis formed an important part of the clothing manufacturing workforce. However they were often concentrated in the least well-paid jobs and physically demanding jobs as machinists and pressers. Many Bengali women worked at home machining. By the early 1980s the Brick Lane clothing industry faced severe competition, particularly from Eastern Europe.[8]

In 2004, the Multi-Fibre Agreement was abolished under the World Trade Organisation Uruguay Round Agreement. As a result Bangladesh saw massive growth of its garment industry.

Ready-made garments are now the leading national export – accounting for around three quarters of annual export receipts and about 10% of GDP. The industry employs between 2.5 and 5.5m million workers depending on how you count them.[9]

A fourth chapter in the history of the East End clothing industry is still being written. There is a wholesale clothes trade with Bengali entrepreneurs and other entrepreneurs from South Asia and Turkey. A trade in Leather manufacture and retail was also established after the Second World War which survives. Brick Lane is becoming a centre for both contemporary fashion and also for selling retro clothing.

Wentworth Street

Wentworth Street is part of the famous Petticoat Lane Sunday Market which started in 1603 with stalls selling lace and silks. If you visit when the market is open and you will spot a wide range of stalls selling leather, fashion and fabrics including printed cottons worn in Africa but usually manufactured in Europe.

Petticoat Lane, 1959 © Tower Hamlets Local History Library and Archives

The colour blue Indigo is a plant-based dye, still widely used to achieve a dark blue colour. Until the mid-20th century, it was the most important form of dye used in India. It was also exported, as it had been for centuries – even as far back as the classical period, when it was a luxury item. As the trade in spices grew in the Middle Ages, so did the trade in indigo, with the dye itself and materials dyed using it becoming available in the markets of London and Amsterdam.

The trade in indigo during the first half of the 19th century involved rivalries between indigo and opium producers, as huge quantities of indigo were passing through Calcutta en route to London.

The production of indigo in Bengal caused the 'Blue Mutiny' of 1859-60, when farmers protested at the poor prices being paid to indigo producers, and the harsh treatment of indigo farmers by the British. The mutiny was one of many events that paved the way towards India's Independence movement.[11]

Indigo factory, Bengal © The British Library Board Shelfmark/Page: WD 1017

An indigo factory in Bengal. Inscribed on front in ink with title and artist's signature. Watercolour. Originally published/produced in 1863. Illustrator: Simpson, William (1823-1899)

The leather trade

Bengali leather and textile wholesalers now trade alongside merchants in cotton and artificial fabrics. The local industry is now shrinking in the face of cheap imports, but wholesale shops dealing in both the leather and clothing trade still dot the bottom of Brick Lane, while the occasional millionaire from the textile industry can still be found in the area. James Caan of Dragon's Den fame, is the son of a Pakistani clothing entrepreneur on Brick Lane.

Jewish tailors' workshop, 1891 © Museum of London

Jewish tailors' workshop an engraving by Ellen Gertrude Cohen. Rooms in ordinary houses in Whitechapel and Spitalfields were often converted into small workshops.

Spitalfields woven silk court dress, 18th century © Museum of London

An example of Spitalfields silk: a court dress dating from the mid-1700s. It is thought to have been made for a Mrs Fanshawe, and was woven from white silk and silver threads, with brocade patterns of flowers and hops (because Mrs Fanshawe's father was a brewer).

The Beauty Clothes Store, Brick Lane, in the 1970s – an example of how the 'rag trade' remained firmly fixed in the East End, despite the changing population. The owner was Abdul Khalique the younger brother of Abdul Jabbar who, at the time, also owned Taj Stores.
© Taj Stores

First phase of large-scale Bengali migration

After the Second World War, in the 1950s and the 1960s, Britain had an economic boom. Unskilled workers were needed. In 1962, the UK government introduced a voucher system, under the Commonwealth Immigration Act, enabling employers to bring in workers from abroad. Many in the Indian sub-continent took this opportunity and used their old links with the settled Asian community. As more jobs were available more and more men came from South Asia to work. [12]

The Bengalis like their counterparts from India and West Pakistan, took this opportunity and used their old links with the settled Bengali community in London. More and more Bengali men came to the UK to earn a living. The Bengali men who came to Britain were generally from rural backgrounds. Their families owned land and were middle-income earners. The men who came to the UK were young, adventurous and were looking for a better life. Their plan was to make a significant amount of money in order to return and settle in Bangladesh but, as we know today, many never did. The present Bengali communities are the descendents of those early settlers.

This 'myth of return', an attitude common to many South Asian settlers, took a long time to dissipate. [13] Gradually, wives and children were brought over to join their husbands and fathers and the 'reality of a permanent British Bengali (Muslim) community had to be recognised.' [14]

In some ways, the wheel has come full circle. For now the production of fabric in the north of England has largely ceased, and today's Bengali community in the East End, like the communities who lived in the area before them, trade in fabric and clothing often made in Asia – frequently in Bangladesh itself. Curiously Dutch Wax (African print) fabrics are still produced in England and sold in many shops on Wentworth Street in Spitalfields.

Chapter 3 - Footnotes

1 Ragged School Museum [online]

2 Knotte and Roche, 2005 [online]

3 Crang, 2005 [online]

4 The British Library [online]

5 GLAADH, 2004

6 The British Library [online]

7 Balfour-Paul, J. (1997 and 1998)

8 Adams, 1994

9 Anwar, 1979

10 Chalmers, 1996, p 5

Chapter 4

Bengali politics in London's East End

More recent history

We have seen how the earliest Bengali political activism in London's East End can be traced to the first Bengali settlers – the seafarers (lascars) – recruited in British India to work for the East India Company. We have also seen how the needs of this early community were at least partially met by the earliest charitable organisations such as the Society for the Protection of Asian Sailors in 1857.

The more recent history of the Bengali community and political activism in London's East End is very much a story of the community taking matters into its own hands.

This started with localised welfare politics, and was later characterised by support for Bangladesh's national independence movement. Later generations of Bengali community activists moved into anti-racist politics, campaigning round community issues such as housing and education, political mobilisation in mainstream politics and the global politics of the anti-war movement.

The 1940s-1950s: Self-help groups and welfare for fellow countrymen

The work of individual Bengalis – such as Ayub Ali Master, with his seamen's café, coffee shop and his use of his own home as an advice centre (see page 38) – was just a beginning.

By the 1950s the Bengali population was growing fast, and with it, the demand for more help and support. The new arrivals – both seamen and others – established the Pakistan Welfare Association – Bangladesh being officially East Pakistan until Independence in 1971.

The Association (now the Bangladesh Welfare Association) still exists, based in a building named Shaheed Bhavan at 39 Fournier Street. The name means 'Martyrs' House and is the largest Bengali community organisation.

It was originally built for the minister of the church in 1750 and was the base of Huguenot charitable work with the local poor. Jewish charities were based here at the end of the 19th century. The Pakistan Welfare Association, formed in 1954, bought this building in the early 1960s. In 1971, as Bangladesh broke away from Pakistan, its name was changed to the Bangladesh Welfare Association and local community leaders pledged their support for an independent Bangladesh.

1960s-1970s: Bangladeshi politics – Liberation War

By the end of 1960s and early 1970s, political developments in Pakistan, and especially in East Pakistan where Bengalis came from, were moving fast. Pakistanis were campaigning against military rule.

In addition the Bengalis of East Pakistan felt that they were getting a raw deal within the framework of Pakistan. As result, resentment grew against the Pakistani ruling elite based in West Pakistan. The cause of East Pakistan was being championed by a party called the Awami League, led by a young charismatic leader, Sheikh Mujibur Rahman.

Many members of London's Bengali community supported Awami League's six-point programme in 1966, which demanded greater autonomy for East Pakistan and they campaigned for Sheikh Mujib's release after he was arrested in 1968. UK Bengalis sent English QC, Sir Thomas Williams to defend Sheikh Mujib and others, who had been charged with treason.

On his release from Pakistan, Sheikh Mujib came to London, on 8 January 1972. He was met by Britain's Prime Minister Edward Heath, Labour Leader Harold Wilson, Peter Shore MP, BBC journalist David Frost, and members of the Steering Committee of the Peoples Republic of Bangladesh. He took up residence at Claridges's Hotel in Mayfair.

In 1971 the Awami League's demand for autonomy had become a fully-fledged Independence War in Bangladesh.

A Bangladesh independence demonstration in Trafalgar Square in 1971. The battle for independence had led to the killing of thousands of Bengalis and the arrest of the elected leader, Sheikh Mujibur Rahman.

Bangladesh independence demonstration in Trafalgar Square, 1971 © Museum of London

During that war, the UK's Bengali community played an important role in highlighting the atrocities taking place in Bangladesh, lobbying the British government and the international community, and raising funds for refugees and Bengali freedom fighters. A key feature of this period was the support provided by members of the white British majority. Among the members of Parliament who gave this support were Michael Barnes, John Stone-house, Bruce Douglas-Mann, and Peter Shore from East London, then MP for Stepney.

For Bengali activists, one of the most important meeting venues at the time was the Dilchad restaurant, near Artillery Lane (an area used long ago for archery and shooting practice by Henry VIII's Honourable Artillery Company). It was here in 1970 that the UK Awami League was formed.

The brothers who own the restaurant (Ataur Rahman Choudhury and Shofiqur Rahman Choudhury) are still involved in community and political activism.

The squatting movement

Housing in the East London has always been very difficult to get. A squatting movement had existed among the white population in east London since around 1968, and from the mid-1970s, Bengalis had also begun to squat – both on their own or with the support of white people.

From late 1974 and early 1975, the Tower Hamlets Squatters' Union and Race Today began actively to campaign amongst the Bengalis over the issues of discrimination over housing.

At the time, the squatters were scattered amongst council flats throughout the area, and there were some streets of squatted houses. These included Aston Street in Stepney, and Nelson and Varden Streets just off New Road. Then, in 1976, a block behind the Montefiore Centre, Hanbury Street, called Pelham Buildings became due for demolition. It contained 60 habitable flats. Mass occupation began on Easter Saturday 1976, with the first seven or eight families. By the end of 1976 there were 300 people in the building.

In January 1976, the Bengali Housing Action Group (BHAG) was formed, giving the issue a formal structure. The Spitalfields Housing and Planning Rights Services (SHAPRS), a legal and housing rights service was established in 1979 and around the same time the Spitalfields Housing Co-op was formed. By the 1980s the business of squatting had become organised and the spontaneity had gone from the movement. However, in terms of generating action, it was 1974-80 that shaped the community the way it is today.

Homeless Families Campaign

Demonstration by Bengali homeless families outside the High Court, 1989 © Tower Hamlets Homeless Families Campaign/Swadhinata Trust

Homeless families from the East End demonstrate outside the High Court in 1989. © Tower Hamlets Homeless Families Campaign/Swadhinata Trust

1978 – the turning point for a new generation

The concern with housing in the 1970s to the 1980s was just one of the ways in which Bengali community politics had moved away from preoccupations with political struggles in Bangladesh to activism in the UK.

From the mid-1970s many British Asians, including Bengalis living in the East End of London, were experiencing racism, social deprivation and high levels of unemployment. The Tower Hamlets Bengali community was under constant attack from the racists from around 1975. For them, the murder of clothing-worker Altab Ali in 1978 was a turning point.

This was especially true for the youth, who became mobilised and politicised. They began to organise youth groups, community and campaigning groups, and linked up with other anti-racist activists. The groups that came out of this struggle included the Bangladesh Youth Movement, Bangladesh Youth Front, Progressive Youth Organisation, Bangladesh Youth Association, and the Bangladesh Youth League.

In the 1980s this second generation of Bengali community activists would enter mainstream politics.

Alliances were forged between some of the first generation and the younger activists. The energy of youth was consolidated by the formation of the Federation of Bangladeshi Youth Organisations (FBYO), an umbrella body, in 1980. It spearheaded campaigns for better housing, health and education and against racism. The FBYO was the first truly national campaigning organisation that represented Bengali interests and spoke for Bengalis across the borough and nationally.

The new generation of activists seized the opportunity to gain both access to the local political system and to various funding streams channelled through the local council, the Greater London Council and the Inner London Education Authority. They also saw the importance of building alliances with activists outside the Bengali community, such as other Asians from Hackney, Newham, Camden, Southall, Birmingham, Bradford, and those from the white majority community of the East End, including Jewish East End activists.

By the 1980s, 34 of the 112 community groups listed by the local education authority were led by Bengalis in Spitalfields ward of Tower Hamlets. As Bengali community activism grew, many activists took prominent roles in community politics and Brick Lane became the centre of Bengali activism.

Around this time, government money began to flow into Spitalfields and other wards where the Bengali population was rapidly expanding, through various 'redevelopment' schemes, such as the Spitalfields Project and Bangladeshi Educational Needs in Tower Hamlets (BENTH), formed in 1983 to pressurise the then Inner London Education Authority to improve educational facilities for the community.

Although it was mostly Bengali men who contributed to these developments, Mithu Ghosh, Pola Uddin, Shila Thakor, Alma Choudhury and Clare Murphy demonstrated the important role played by women and the influence of debates about women's rights and gender equality. In 1970s Anwara Haq formed Nari Samity (1978). and Mrs Fakharuddin formed the Mahila Samity. Mrs Lily Khan and Lulu Bilkis Banu were also active at the time. The Jagonari Women's Education Resource Centre was built by an Asian women's collective in the 1980s. [1]

Jagonari Centre, Whitechapel. 2010 © Kois Miah/Swadhinata Trust

WUAR – Women Unite Against Racism 1993-1995

The involvement of women in local politics increased after the racist attack on student Quddus Ali, on 8 September 1993 and the election of the BNP councillor Derek Beackon in Millwall Ward on 16 September 1993. Women United Against Racism (WUAR) was formed in 1993 at a conference in Tower Hamlets College. The women were angry at the election of the BNP councillor and felt excluded from the anti-racist movement dominated by men. WUAR was a unique alliance of local women, including but not exclusively Bengali women.

The organisation contributed significantly to the defeat of the BNP in Tower Hamlets by ensuring women registered to vote and encouraging women to vote in the election. WUAR also took part in anti-racist activities, meetings and rallies demonstrating the importance of women from diverse background working together against racism and sexism.

A poster asking for public assistance in finding the murderers of Altab Ali, in 1978. © Paul Trevor

March with Altab Ali's coffin © Paul Trevor

Marchers accompany Altab Ali's coffin, 1978.

© Paul Trevor

Women Unite Against Racism demonstrate in the late 1970s.

© Julie Begum/WUAR

Racism in the East End

Altab Ali was far from being the only Bengali victim of racism in the East End. In 1970, Tosir Ali was murdered by racists in Aldgate, and in 1978 Ishaq Ali was stabbed to death by racists in Hackney. Racial violence began to escalate again against the Bengalis and other ethnic groups during 1993 when the British National Party won a council seat in the Isle of Dogs. In 1993 Quddus Ali, a 17-year-old Bengali student at Tower Hamlets College was savagely beaten by a group of white men, including skinheads, outside a pub near Watney Market. In 1994 Muktar Ahmed, 19, was severely beaten by a gang of 20 white youths in Bethnal Green. In 2001 Shiblu Rahman was stabbed to death in Bow outside his own flat.

However, the community has resisted racism and when the British National Party started to sell their newspapers in Brick Lane, Bengali community and anti-racist demonstrations forced them to abandon their paper-selling pitch at the junction of Brick Lane and Bethnal Green Road.

As the accounts above demonstrate alongside Bengali organisations have been a variety of anti-racist organisations. There have been a series of community relations councils starting with the Council of Citizens of East London formed in the 1930s, the Council of Citizens of Tower Hamlets formed in 1965, later Tower Hamlets Council for Racial Equality (THCRE), THARJ - Tower Hamlets Association for Racial Justice (1980), THCRE - Tower Hamlets Council for Racial Equality, Tower Hamlets Race Equality Council and THARE - Tower Hamlets Association for Racial Equality. There have been anti-racist groups more or less aligned with political parties such as the Anti-Nazi League (Socialist Workers Party, Militant and others) and East London Workers Against Racism (the Revolutionary Communist Party), the Anti Racist Alliance (the Labour Party and TUC), National assembly Against Racism (Labour Party and Trade Unions). There have also been campaigns round specific issues such as those round housing and homelessness –the Campaign to Clear Hostels and Slums, Tower Hamlets Squatters Union, Faceless Homeless, Bengali Housing Action Group and the Homeless Families Campaign.

The changing community

A new generation of Bengalis is growing up. Many are highly educated and tend to pull away from those without prospects and are ready to contribute to the crucial economic and social changes in the East End.

These changes have included the gradual decline of the garment-manufacturing sector due to cheap imports (see Chapter 3, page 45) and the growth of the service sector, especially restaurants and shops. 'Banglatown' (the area around Brick Lane where there is a large Bengali population) has become a global icon – a branding concept – and the 'curry capital of Europe'.

In Spitalfields, the impact of the 'global city' has been felt by the Bengali community as local conservation areas were gentrified by rich, mainly white incomers. The area became a base for high technology, advertising, media and the arts, while City of London businesses also moved into the area.

Across the borough, the derelict docks in the south have been transformed into the gleaming Manhattan-style landscape of Canary Wharf. Expensive housing – in effect, for white middle class newcomers – has been built on the Isle of Dogs and other southern localities.

Mainstream politics

1982 saw the first Bengali elected to Tower Hamlets Council. Nurul Huque, an independent candidate from Spitalfields, became a councillor, defeating a Labour candidate. He was followed by Ashik Ali, a Labour candidate, who became a councillor in St Katherine's ward. Today, Tower Hamlets Council has the largest number of Black, Asian or Bengali councillors in the country.

A step into the future

All the parliamentary candidates from Bethnal Green and Bow for the 2010 General election (Labour, Conservative, Liberal Democrat, Respect and Green parties) were Bengalis, with the result that the first Bengali entered the House of Commons that year – the Labour candidate Rushanara Ali.

Two women

Pola Uddin

Baroness Uddin

Pola Uddin was made a member of the House of Lords as one of Tony Blair's 'working peers' in 1998, in recognition of her contribution to the advancement of women and disability rights. [2]

She started her professional career by creating and leading community working groups in the late 1970s. In the early 1980s she was involved in building the first purpose-built education and training centre for Asian women in the UK called the Jagonari Centre, located a Whitechapel, East London completed in 1986. She was a liaison officer with Tower Hamlets Social services and then a manager of a Tower Hamlets Women's Health Project. In 1988, she started working for Newham social services. In 1990, she was elected a Labour councillor in the London Borough of Tower Hamlets, the first Bengali woman to hold such an office in a local authority in the United Kingdom. After serving for two years, she became the Deputy Leader of Tower Hamlets council, from 1994 to 1996.

In 1997, she applied to be a candidate for the Bethnal Green and Bow constituency, but did not reach the shortlist. She became Baroness Uddin, of Bethnal Green in the London Borough of Tower Hamlets – the youngest woman on the benches and was the first and only Bengali woman to be appointed to the House of Lords.

Rushanara Ali

Rushanara Ali has made history by becoming the first Bengali to enter House of Commons in 2010. Rushanara Ali grew up in Tower Hamlets, having moved to the UK from Bangladesh when she was seven years old. She studied at Mulberry School and Tower Hamlets College before gaining a place at Oxford University.

She worked on human rights issues at the Foreign Office from 2000-2001. Prior to this, she was a Research Fellow at the Institute of Public Policy Research (IPPR) focusing on anti-discrimination issues from 1999-2002. From 2002-2005, she worked at the Communities Directorate of the Home Office, in the aftermath of the 2001 disturbances in Burnley, Bradford and Oldham, to prevent further conflict and unrest. She was an Associate Director of the Young Foundation in Bethnal Green.

She has also been Chair of Tower Hamlets Summer University, a commissioner on the London Child Poverty Commission, a Board Member of Tower Hamlets College, Trustee of the Paul Hamlyn Foundation and member of the Tate Britain Council.[3]

Rushanara Ali

Some of the major Bengali organisations that operate, or have operated in the East End

In 2010 these included

Business

- Bangladesh Caterers Association
- Bangladesh British Chamber of Commerce
- Brick Lane Business Association
- Banglatown Restaurant Association

Political

- Awami League
- Bangladesh Nationalist Party
- Jatiya Party
- JSD (Jatiya Samajtantrik Dal)
- BSD (Bangladesher Samajtantrik Dal)
- CPB (Communist Party of Bangladesh)
- Workers Party of Bangladesh

Faith organisations and places of worship

Brick Lane Jamme Masjid – (Brick Lane Mosque)

The Brick Lane Mosque at no 59 has been a place of worship for 250 years. It was built in 1743 by French-speaking Protestant Huguenot refugees, who named it La Neuve Eglise, or 'the New Church'. In 1809 it was leased to the London Society for promoting Christianity among the Jews and was called the Jews Chapel. Then, in 1819 it became a Wesleyan Methodist Church. In 1897 it was bought by the Jewish ultra-Orthodox immigrant Machzikei Hadath society and became an orthodox Jewish Synagogue in 1898, called the Spitalfields Great Synagogue.

Brick Lane Synagogue, n.d. (Press Cuttings Collection, Bishopsgate Library)

In 1976 it became East London's second mosque and is considered to be Bengali Muslims' central mosque. The building houses a religious school on the first floor.

High above, on the Fournier Street side of the building is the sundial bearing the mournful Latin message umbra sumus – 'we are shadows'. This is probably taken from the Roman poet Horace, who wrote that we are only dust and shadow – a reference to things always changing as day changes to night and the seasons change. It is an appropriate motto for a building whose purpose has changed over the years, but which has remained a centre for worship. The words have recently been used by the Stepney-born musician Jah Wobble, a former associate of the Sex Pistols and bass player with Public Image Limited, for a song and album title. Judith Weir, the classical composer and former Artistic Director of the Spitalfields Festival, also used it.

The building is Grade II listed, and includes cellars originally for commercial storage, now part of the prayer hall of the mosque, and an adjoining schoolhouse and offices. It actually comprises two distinct structures, the main building facing the South towards Fournier Street, (the former church and synagogue, and now the main prayer hall) and an adjoining building with its entrance at Brick Lane. When the building became a mosque in 1976, minor alterations were made to the interior, pews and other non-structural fittings were removed and a qibla was constructed on the ground floor facing east towards Makkah (Mecca).

In 2010, an eye-catching 30-metre illuminated steel minaret-like structure was erected at the corner of Brick Lane and Fournier Street.

Brick Lane Mosque with the tower. Courtesy Altyerre 2010

The building that is now a mosque operated as a synagogue for many years, right into the middle of the 20th century. Here it is shown at the turn of the 19th and 20th centuries.

Spitalfields Great Synagogue © London Metropolitan Archives

The same building in the 1950s, when there was still a large Jewish population in the East End.

Spitalfields Great Synagogue, 1951 © London Metropolitan Archives

The interior of the Great Synagogue in 1951.

© London Metropolitan Archives

The much-changed interior of the building that was once the Great Synagogue, and which is now the Brick Lane Mosque.

The interior today as a mosque, 2010 © Altyerre

Another view of the inside of the Brick Lane Mosque. A few of the original features of the building when it was a church and then a synagogue can still be seen.

The interior today as a mosque, 2010 © Altyerre

East London Mosque

In 1910 a group of prominent British Muslims, including Lord Headley (who had converted to Islam in 1896, while working in India as a civil engineer), and Syed Ameer Ali formally established the London Mosque Fund, to finance a mosque in London. In 1940, the East London Mosque Trust purchased houses in 446-448 Commercial Road to run as a mosque. It was opened in 1941 as the East London Mosque and Islamic Cultural Centre.

Then, in 1975, the Greater London Council acquired the premises in Commercial Road under a compulsory purchase order. Temporary buildings were provided until in the 1980s the East London Mosque moved to its present site. The present mosque was opened in 1985, complete with dome and minarets.

The site of the original East London Mosque in Commercial Road. 1972 © Tower Hamlets Local History Library and Archives

East London Mosque current site, 1980s © Tower Hamlets Local History Library and Archives

The Markazi Mosque has been in use for worship by Muslims since 1980.

The building dates from 1929 when the Christian Street Synagogue or Talmud Torah Synagogue moved out.

The Bengali Christian Fellowship

Christ Church on Commercial Street was designed by Nicholas Hawksmoor and built in 1729, to impress local people with state and religious authority and show them that Anglicanism was the most heavenly of Christian denominations. It is now home to the Bengali Christian Fellowship, which dates from 1978. Its membership, which runs into hundreds, lives mainly in the East End, but is also drawn from other parts of London. Its members come from a variety of Christian backgrounds, ranging from Roman Catholic to evangelical groups.

The Fellowship's primary function is to provide Christian fellowship and instruction for Bengali-speaking Christians. Larger meetings are held at Christ Church and smaller ones at Lincoln Road Chapel in Ponders End. Meetings also take place in homes for Bible study. There has been partnership with Bangla TV to produce Christian programmes to broadcast during Christmas and Easter, in addition to distributing audio-visual materials in Bengali.

Joint fellowship at Christ Church, Spitalfields 2009

Bengali Christian fellowship at Christ Church Spitalfields

Christmas celebration 2009
© Swadhinata Trust Photo Ansar Ahmed Ullah

*Christian services and other activities take place in a beautifully refurbished
church that was originally designed in the 18th century for Anglicans, by
Nicholas Hawksmoor (1661-1736).*

Christ Church, Spitalfields. 2010 © Kois Miah/Swadhinata Trust

The Hindu community

In addition to Christians and a small number of Bengali Buddhists, there is a significant minority community (numbering about 4,500) of Hindus. In 1977 they formed Hindu Pragati Sangha to foster religious practice and cultural traditions and, in 1985, acquired a permanent place, 33 Rhondda Grove, Mile End. Plans are now in train to construct Tower Hamlets' first Bengali Hindu temple, Hindu Pragati Mandir.

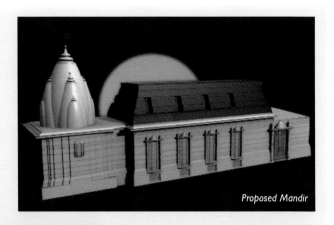

Proposed Mandir

The Sanaton Association was established in the London Borough of Tower Hamlets in 1983 to support the social, cultural, educational and welfare needs of the Bengali Hindu Community. In plays an important part in celebrating the Bengali New Year, the Hindu Spring, Winter and Autumn festivals and cultural events, which are mainly organised at Toynbee Hall and other community centres in the borough. The Sanaton Association also offers supplementary education to children. [4]

'Saraswati Puja', the ritual worship of Saraswati, the Hindu goddess of wisdom and knowledge. This takes place annually, on a day known as Vasant Panchami.

Saraswati Puja, 2010 © Swadhinata Trust

There is a small population of Bengali Buddhists in London, numbering a few hundred.

Puja celebration, 2009 © Sanaton Association

Chapter 4 - Footnotes

1 Jagonari Women's Education Resource Centre [online]

2 BritBangla 2002-3 [online]

3 Rushanara Ali, 2008 [online]

4 Sanaton Association 2007

Chapter 5

Education

A long tradition

The East End has a long tradition of supplementary education. For Jewish young people, there were cheders for religious and language teaching, and also secular radical night schools, at which volunteers taught young immigrants who had little or no formal education.

For the Bengali community, too, supplementary education began with religion, starting at the East London Mosque in the 1960s. With the arrival of families in the 1970s, similar classes were set up elsewhere, run by volunteers.

East End Community School

In 1977, some members of the Bengali community decided that a new approach to supplementary education was necessary. Mrs Anwara Begum and Mr Muhammad Nurul Huque headed a group of parents, who were concerned at the children's lack of access to their own language and culture. They decided to open a new school in a damp derelict two-roomed basement flat at 269 Brunswick Buildings, New Goulston Street, E1 (now demolished).

In 1980, the school was moved to its new premises, made up of Portakabins on Old Castle Street behind the Denning Point tower block. Originally a temporary home for the school, it is still there more than 30 years later.

The East End Community School inspired other schools in Tower Hamlets and throughout East End and beyond. There are at least 90 Bengali supplementary schools in Tower Hamlets,[1] including state-run schools providing Bengali language classes.

Some local schools with Bengali names

Shapla Primary School (named after Bangladesh's national flower, Shapla – a water lily) opened in Wellclose Square in 1987. It is a one-form entry primary school catering for pupils from a wide range of social backgrounds who live in and around Shadwell in Tower Hamlets. [2]

Kobi Nazrul Primary School (named after Bangladesh's national poet Kazi Nazrul Islam), in Settles Street. It opened in 1996.[3]

Bangabandhu Primary School, (named after Bangladesh's founder Bangabandhu Sheikh Mujibur Rahman) in Wessex Street. It opened in 1991 on its current site but was operating from Wessex Centre from 1989. [4]

Osmani primary school, (named after the Commander of Bengali freedom fighters Col M A G Osmani) at Vallance Road opened in 1986.

Shapla School, Cable Street 2010
© Swadhinata Trust. Photo Kois Miah

Kobi Nazrul Primary School, Settles Street 2010
© Swadhinata Trust. Photo Kois Miah

Bangabandhu School, Wessex Street. 2010
© Kois Miah/Swadhinata Trust

Osmani School, Vallance Road. 2010
© Kois Miah/Swadhinata Trust

Christchurch School

Ninety-five per cent of the pupils at Christchurch Church of England Primary School are Bengali Muslims. A century ago, when Stepney's Jewish population was 120,000, they would have been 95 per cent Jewish.

Originally built as the Parish School, the school attempts to reassure the Jewish community that their children were safe and welcome is still evident in the Star of David at the top of a drainpipe on the front of the building.
After school, many of the children go along to the Brick Lane Mosque for religious teaching and Bengali lessons until about 7pm, just as their Jewish predecessors would have had after-school hours learning about their culture and religion.

Christ Church School, Brick Lane. 2010 © Kois Miah/Swadhinata Trust

Chapter 5 - Footnotes

1 Huque, 2009

2 Shapla Primary School [online]

3 Kobi Nazrul Primary School [online]

4 Bangabandhu Primary School [online]

Chapter 6

Food and tea

Europeans and Indian workers on
a tea plantation in Darjeeling -
West Bengal - East India, 1860 -70
© Royal Geographical Society
(with IBG)

Kolkata (Calcutta) was founded by Job Charnock, an English sailor, who settled in a Bengali village 240km up the river Hooghly in 1687. It soon became an East India Company trading post and fort, and grew into a great port city, from where the Sylhet seamen mostly sailed. They were, as we have seen, the forebears of today's East End Bengali community.

At first The East India Company shipped thousands of tonnes of tea to Britain from China. In 1824, Robert and Charles Bruce, two brothers from Scotland, discovered wild tea growing in Assam. However, it was not immediately recognised as such: the curator of the Botanical Gardens, a medical doctor called Nathan Wolff – thought it was another member of the Camellia family. It was not until 1835 that he accepted it was tea.

In 1840, a tea garden was established in Chittagong. By 1855, wild tea plants were also discovered at Chandkhani Hills of Sylhet in Bangladesh.

The first commercial tea garden in Bangladesh was, however, established in 1857 at Malnicherra Tea Estate, two miles away from Sylhet town.[1]

From the 1850s tea was exported from Assam (now in India) and from British tea estates on the hills of Sylhet, (now Bangladesh). It all went through Calcutta. Thus, a strong link between Calcutta and the East End was established – and signs of this remain to this day.

One of these signs is Calcutta House, situated in Old Castle Street on the corner of Whitechapel High Street. The building belonged to the Brooke Bond Tea Company (now part of Unilever), but is now used by London Metropolitan University. The East India Company owned tea warehouses in Cutler Street (where tea from Ceylon – Sri Lanka – was mainly stored) and Commercial Road, where Indian teas were kept.
Tetley's (now owned by the Indian Tata Corporation) had a warehouse at the top of Commercial Road too.

Lipton's (also part of Unilever) had its tea warehouse on the corner of Bethnal Green Road and Shoreditch High Street. It is now a fashionable meeting place for young people.
© *Ken Russell*

The warehouses belonging to tea merchants Kearly and Tonge. Like other tea merchants, the firm imported from Bengal.
© *Ken Russell)*

The first restaurants

In 1809, the first establishment to serve Indian food was the
Hindostanee Coffee House at 34 George Street, Portman
Square, London. It was opened by Dean Mahomed from
Patna, Bihar, India. He offered a house 'for the Nobility and
Gentry where they might enjoy the Hookha with real
Chilm tobacco and Indian dishes of the highest perfection'. [2]
The decor was very colonial, with bamboo chairs and
picture-decked walls. Unfortunately, as outgoings were greater
than incomings, Mahomed had to file for bankruptcy
in 1812. However, the restaurant managed to carry on
without him in some form until 1833. [3]

The first recorded Indian restaurant in the 20th century
was the Salut e Hind in Holborn in 1911. [4]

Home is not home without Home and Colonial Tea, 1932-1937
© *Museum of London*

'Home is not home without Home and Colonial Tea, so buy
your tea at the H&C: a picture of two cooks carrying a box
of tea.' This billboard poster advertises tea sold by the
Home and Colonial chain of grocery stores. It was designed
and produced by Benson's London advertising agency.

Tea imported from India and Sri Lanka (Ceylon) was sent direct from Tilbury Docks by rail to Commercial Road warehouses, where there was over 100,000 sq metres of storage.

Tea on a conveyer system, Tilbury Docks, 1920 © Museum of London Photograph: John Avery (Museum of London)

A fashionably dressed family takes tea under the shade of a large tree as waiter behind them fills a teapot. The children play with toys and a dog and the table is laid with a china tea service. This image marks the point when tea-drinking was no longer the confined to the rich, and was on its way to becoming the British national drink.

A Tea Garden, 1790 © Museum of London

Unloading tea from ships at East India Docks in 1867. Many of the sailors who carried this cargo to London would have been Bengalis.

Unloading tea-ships in the East India Docks, 1867 © Tower Hamlets Local History Library and Archives

Thomas Lipton lived at Osidge, in Southgate, north London. This photograph taken around 1900 shows the family in a tree house in the garden, waited on by an Indian servant.

© London Borough of Enfield

Between the wars

Mohammed Wayseem and Mohammed Rahim, from northern India, opened the Shafi café in 1920 in London's Gerrard Street in Chinatown, employing four or five ex-seamen. It soon became a kind of community and Indian Student Centre. The numbers of Indian students in the UK rose from 100 in 1880 to 1800 by 1931.

Soon the Shafi was taken over by Dharam Lal Bodua and run by an English manager with Bengali employees, including Israil Miah and Gofur Miah, who were later to run their own establishments. Bengali, Ayub Ali Master opened a curry café at 76 Commercial Street, London, in the 1920s.[5]

Other establishments for the seamen, usually from the province of Sylhet, Bangladesh, opened throughout the years between the wars, such as Abdul Rashim and Koni Khan's coffee shop, serving curry and rice on Victoria Dock Road around 1920.[6]

Many other cafés opened around the seaports of Britain by ex-seamen but all had great difficulty in obtaining the necessary rice and spices.

Fashionable restaurants

The early twentieth century restaurants were, not surprisingly, mainly for Asians but, in 1927, the first fashionable Indian restaurant opened when Edward Palmer opened Veeraswamy's Indian Restaurant in London's Regent Street where it still thrives today.

Gradually, the number of Indian restaurants increased. Among the early establishments in the West End were The Durbar on Percy Street, owned by Asuk Mukerjee from Calcutta, and The Dilkush in Windmill Street, owned by Nogandro Goush, also from Calcutta. A Punjabi, Asif Khan, owned the Shalimar on Wardour Street and Jobbul Haque of Urisya was proprietor of The Bengal India – like the Durbar, on Percy Street.

In the East End, Abdul Gofur ran a café shop at 120 Brick Lane, and similar establishments existed in New Road and Commercial Road. In 1938, on his return from a trip to America, Ayub Ali Master opened The Shah Jalal at 76 Commercial Street London. Shirref's in Great Castle Street opened in 1935 and Halal, which still thrives today, opened in St Marks Street E1 in 1939.[7]

During and after Second World War

During the Second World War, restaurants continued to open away from the East End – for example the Gathor, a basement cafe (once again, in Percy Street in the West End) and Sanu Miah's Green Mask on Brompton Road. This last became a centre for prominent East Pakistanis (now Bengalis), including politicians. Also in 1942–3 Mosrof Ali and Israil Miah opened The Anglo Asian at 146 Brompton Road, London and by 1957 Mosrof Ali also had The Durbar in Hareford Road. His last business was the Curry Garden in 1975, which he set up before retiring in 1979.[8]

By one account, there were 20 so-called 'Indian' restaurants in London by 1946. These included the Halal Restaurant, situated in the East End off Alie Street. It opened in 1939, and was reputedly the first proper Asian restaurant in the area.

Amongst the first coffee houses offering curries in East London was one adjacent to the first East London Mosque, which opened in 1941 at 448 Commercial Road and another in Whitechurch Lane. Such places were more than simply food outlets – Moktar Ali's café on Cable Street was also a key meeting place for local Bengali seamen seeking company and support, as was a café on 118 Commercial Street (which is still a restaurant).[9]

A Punjabi café which was part of the Gower's Walk Hindustani Community House (now demolished) established by Kunder Lal Jalie in 1937 also held a position of importance. It was the place where Jinnah came to secure a vote of confidence for his future government of Pakistan from what was then the 'East Bengali' community in East London.[10]

A major industry

In 1960, there were just 500 Indian restaurants in Britain but by 1970, this had grown to 1200.

By the 1980s numbers of Indian restaurants in Britain had reached about 3000, and by 2000 there were around 8000. Today the Indian food sector in the UK has an annual turnover of £4.3 billion, in the form of 9,500 Indian restaurants and takeaways, and employs at least 70,000 people – more than coal, steel and shipbuilding combined. In fact, the trade has become one of the major industries in the UK – and has taken on a particularly British character.
Chicken Tikka Masala, a British-Bengali creation has become so popular that statistics show that nearly 15 per cent of all first choices in restaurants are for this dish – which is unknown in the sub-continent.[11]

From ship's cooks to chefs

The success story of the so-called 'Indian' restaurants in the UK is all the more remarkable for the fact that almost all the early cafés were set up, owned and run by ship's cooks. As we have seen now they can often be found even in the grandest, smartest neighbourhoods and clusters of curry houses are magnets for visitors in all Britain's major cities. Yet today, it is still Brick Lane – Banglatown, the heartland of UK's Bengali community – which is known as 'the curry capital of Europe'. It has over 50 restaurants (up from 24 in 1997). This is the largest cluster of Indian restaurants and cafes in the UK, and supplies Indian/Bengali/Pakistani food both to customers from across London's communities – both white and ethnic minority. The owners of the restaurants and cafes in Brick Lane and the workforce of around 500 are almost exclusively Bengali.[12]

Estimates of what proportion of Indian restaurants are from Bangladesh – vary – between 80 and 95%. The proportion of Bangladeshis compared to Asians in Britain generally is less than one in five people.[13] Like their forebears, the lascars, they mostly originate from Sylhet.

The food

Many of the smaller cafés offer a more authentically Bengali range of dishes – the sort of food people cook in their homes. Given its geography, it is not surprising that fish is popular in Bangladesh – delicious bhorta, curries made from river fish such as koi, or ocean fish, such as pomfret, cooked in fiery spices, onions and garlic, or steaks of cod-like boal, served with beans. Meat and lamb are eaten, too, along with potatoes (sometimes made into cutlets) or served with a purée of lentils. Snacks – often sold at roadside tea-stalls – include shingara – a crisp pastry with a filling of spiced potato, a little like samosas, but rounder. Sweet dishes may be yoghurt-based mishti doi or vapa pitha. Cafés may also offer borhani, a yoghurt-based drink normally only served at weddings.[14]

Some of the first restaurants in and around Brick Lane

- Sonar Bangla was operating at 46 Hanbury Street from 1968, before that, its basement had been used as a mosque. Sonar Bangla was established by Redwanul Haque who had come to the UK in 1959. In 1971 the restaurant was used to drum up support for Bangladesh independence movement. It closed in 1995.
- Nazrul, set up in 1971, claims to be the oldest Bengali restaurant on Brick Lane.
- Meraz Café on Hanbury Street opened in 1974.
- Dilchad was founded by Choudhury family in 1962. At the time the restaurant rapidly became a popular meeting place for Bengali students, politicians and community activists. The restaurant now is one of the most successful Bengali owned restaurants in the area and serves Persian, Afghan, Arab and English-influenced Bengali food.

Bengali food

A range of foods that might seem very exotic outside the Bengali community can be found in Bengali grocery shops. These include frozen freshwater fish from Bangladesh's haors (flooded fields) or the rivers such as the Ganges and Brahmaputra that lace Bangladesh. Boal is one of these fish, as are ruhi – mirror carp; bhag – a large leopard spotted fish; tasty little keshki; delicious oily ilish (or hilsa); dried fish, or shidol, a pungent fish. Vegetables include white radish, okra, sheem beans, shatkora, a bitter lemony fruit of Sylhet, jhinga (ribbed sponge gourd), chalkumra, misti kumra (pumpkins), kala thur (banana flower) and all sorts of saag (spinach).[15]

Taj Stores – first Bengali grocery shop

The first Bengali grocery shop, Taj Stores, was opened in 1936 in Hunton Street (now known as Buxton Street, near Allen Gardens) by a Bengali seaman, Abdul Jabbar, who had come to the UK in 1934. It has moved a number of times since then and can now be found at 112 Brick Lane, where it is still run and managed by members of Abdul Jabbar's family.[16]

The late Mr Abdul Jabbar, in the 1960s. He was the brother of Abdul Kalique, who came to the UK as a seaman and opened Taj Stores.
© *Taj Stores*

The Taj Stores on Hunton Street, in 1936. In this picture, from, left to right are Muhammad Bashir Miah and Abdul Khalique. © *Taj Stores*

Abdul Khalique and a younger
brother, Abdul Rahman in a
picture taken in the 1960s
© *Taj Stores*

The second location of Taj Stores at 109 Brick Lane, in the early 1980s
© *Taj Stores*

Inside the Taj Stores at 109 Brick Lane. From left to right: Kaysor Miah and Komrow Uddin
© *Taj Stores*

The Taj Mahal Restaurant, one of the first proper restaurants, at 105 Brick Lane. It had previously been 'Sweet Heaven' – a restaurant serving snacks and Bengali sweets
© *Taj Stores*

Taj Stores current site, Brick Lane. 2010
© *Kois Miah/Swadhinata Trust*

Ali Brothers, Fashion Street. 2010 © Kois Miah/Swadhinata Trust

One of the other older grocery shops in Banglatown area is run
by the Ali Brothers in Fashion Street which opened in 1970.

The community grows

By 1940, the community of Bengali residents in London had grown to around 300.
Then, in around 1956, the existing community of seamen was joined by another
2-3000 adventurers. Nawab Ali, who owned a coffee shop at 11 Settles Street,
near the Labour Exchange, said 'they just used to show up with my name in a taxi
– at one point, my wife went crazy – there were 35 of them living upstairs!'[17]
Later, Nawab Ali also had the Commonwealth Club, in Umberston Street, and a
butcher's shop in Hessel Street, now run by his son.

The first local halal butcher's opened as long ago as 1940: a sign that a Muslim
community was settling into the area. The proprietor was Taslim Ali, who later
became Imam of the East London Mosque.[18] The family now runs the
undertakers' service at Whitechapel's East London Mosque.

Chapter 6 - Footnotes

1 Grove [online]

2 Grove [online]

3 Indian catering [online]

4 Visram, 2002

5 History of 'Indian' Restaurants and Curry Houses in Britain [online]

6 New Statesman [online]

6 History of 'Indian' Restaurants and Curry Houses in Britain [online]

7 'History of 'Indian' Restaurants and Curry Houses in Britain [online]

8 Adams, 1987

9 Sokoloff, 1987

10 Grove, 2009 [online]

11 Carey, 2004

12 Time Out, No 1920

13 Jones, 2004

14 A Brief History of Taj Stores, 2006

15 Lamarche, 2003

16 Adams, 1987

Chapter 7

The community now

Why the East End?

Immigrants settled in the East End of London, close to the Brick Lane/Banglatown area, because living costs there were relatively cheap and job prospects made the area particularly attractive.

We saw on page 44 how the first wave of immigration arrived from France in the late 1500s, with the French Huguenot Protestants fleeing persecution by migrating to London from the late seventeenth century onwards. (The word 'refugee' entered the English language at this time.) Both as a result of prosperity and poverty (when imports from India among other places shrank demand for their textiles), they moved to other parts of the UK. However they were followed by other waves of immigrants: the Irish escaping during the great 'potato famine' of the 1840s, followed by the Eastern European Jews.

Jewish community

The first Jews to settle in the East End were the prosperous Sephardim Jews who had fled to other countries from the Inquisition from Spain and Portugal and were later permitted to enter England in 1656. But the largest influx of Jews arrived after fleeing pogroms following the assassination of Tsar Alexander in 1881.

There were anti-Jewish riots in the province of Kherson, bloody pogroms in Kiev and Odessa and the disorders spread to Poland, in Warsaw too ... some 200 Jewish communities had been subjected to murder, arson, pillage and rape. The Jewish community who came to the East End settled in Aldgate, Commercial Street and eastwards past Brick Lane into Commercial Road, Mile End, Bethnal Green as well as Cable Street. The Jews worked in and soon dominated the sweatshops, furniture making, tobacco, leather goods, shoe making and tailoring sector. In 1901 over 40 per cent of London's Jewish men worked in the garment industry. In 1914 the Jewish population of East London estimated at 180,000[1]

Many Jews, however, saw the East End as only a temporary home, America was the promised land. Of those who stayed, the majority eventually moved out of the East End to more affluent areas of North London and Essex, where they established large communities. Gradually, synagogues closed, and shops and factories were taken over by new immigrants; the Bengalis from the then East Pakistan and now Bangladesh. [2]

Many of the new arrivals from Russia and East European countries settled in Tower Hamlets. Between 1880 and the First World War 100,000 Jews had settled in the East End of London. By 1900, most local shops and markets were Jewish. By 1914, there were around 150,000 Jews living in the Whitechapel and Aldgate area alone. More Jews arrived in the 1930s as refugees from the Nazis though very few of these refugees settled in the East End. Today there are fewer than 2,000 Jews in all of Tower Hamlets and the population is dwindling. [3]

This pattern of migration out of the area had been true for centuries. As the Jews left, they made way for Bengalis.

The formation of a close-knit community helped the immigrants in migrating and settling. Racial tension between Bengalis and established white British communities was evident in a rise in racial violence which, in turn, resulted in the Bengali community becoming even more close-knit, as it settled in an unfamiliar and hostile environment. The fear of violence in other parts of the UK meant there was an influx of new immigrants to this already populated area of the East End. Research indicates that this kind of movement is commonplace — to avoid racial harassment, ethnic groups tend to find solidarity within their own communities and that 'ethnic density' can act as a protective factor in physical and mental health.

The second phase of settlement: women and children arrive

By the 1970s, most men realised that they would perhaps be staying here longer than they had originally expected to. When Bangladesh became independent in 1971, the long haul flight to the UK and the bureaucracy to obtain travel papers were reduced (instead of travelling from Dhaka – East Pakistan to Karachi – West Pakistan and then to the UK, families could come to the UK direct from Dhaka). Many families took this opportunity to make the journey to join their men-folk in Britain.

With the arrival of the families, the Bengali community began to grow, and there are now up to 350,000 people of Bengali origin living in England, making it the largest community outside of Bangladesh. [4]

Today there are 180,000 Bengalis living in London. [5] More than half are residents of three inner London boroughs: Tower Hamlets, Newham and Camden. This marks a significant change from the early days when Bengali seamen, if they found wives at all, married local women. The social historian, Yousuf Choudhury, writes, 'In 1957 a number of Sylheti (Bengalis) were married and had children from their white wives. Hardly any Sylheti women were to be seen …' [6]

British born Bengalis of mixed heritage (Anglo-Indian or Eurasian) tended to assimilate into white British society through marriage, thus there never was a permanent British Bengali community until Bengali women began arriving in large numbers from 1970s. [7]

A Bengali family portrait taken in Verdi photographers studios in Green Street in the late 1970s.
In picture, we can see: Mr Annar Miah, Mrs Rajahan Begum, Akther Miah and Nurjahan Julie Begum
© Julie Begum

A typical family portrait taken in the 1970s, at a time when Bengalis were beginning to settle in the East End as families.

Branch Road, E14, 1982 children in street
© Tower Hamlets Local History Library and Archives

Children play outside their homes near Brick Lane, 1983 © Museum of London

Photographer Henry Grant captured these children playing in the streets and narrow external stairwells outside their homes in the East End in the 1980s. (A fenced area of land beside the low-rise flats provided some space for ball games.) By this time, the Bengali community had become settled in the area.

Banglatown 1997

'Banglatown' is now the official name for Brick Lane and the surrounding area. This happened in 1997, after a campaign among local community activists aimed at getting recognition for the largest Bengali settlement in the UK. In 2001, the electoral ward of Spitalfields was renamed as Spitalfields and Banglatown Ward.

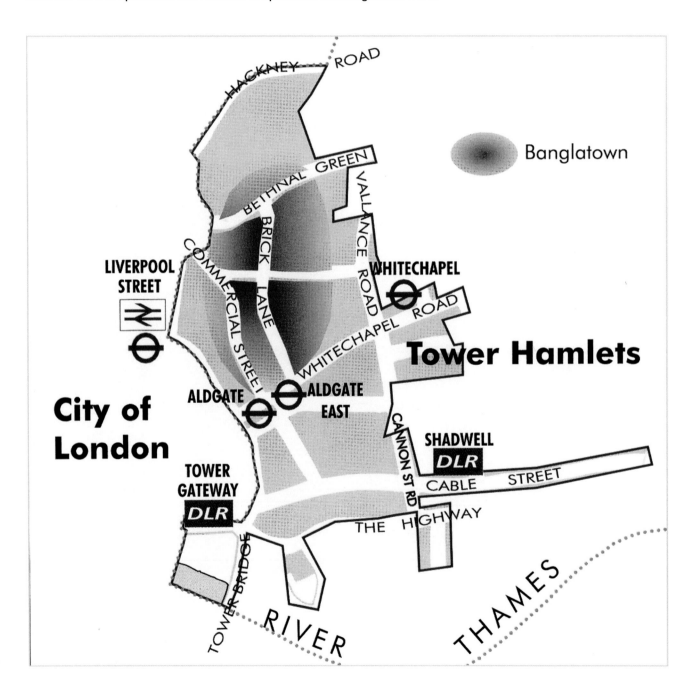

Chapter 7 - Footnotes

1 Lipman, 1954, p 85 - 108

2 Taylor, 2004, p146

3 Tower Hamlets Inter Faith Forum

4 Greater London Authority, 2009

5 Choudhury, 1993, p 136

6 Fisher, 2006

Chapter 8

Some landmarks

Altab Ali Park

Many roads and buildings in 'Banglatown' illustrate the area's long history – and its connections with the Indian sub-continent. Commercial Road, for example, was built to enable the East India Company to transport its goods from the docks to their warehouses. This road crosses Whitechapel High Street (where the famous Whitechapel Art Gallery has been since 1902).

A little way along this street, there is an open space – once a churchyard – lying between Whitechurch Lane and Adler Street. This had been attached first to the 'White chapel' that stood there in the 13th century. It gave way in 1338 to a parish church called St Mary Matfelon which was damaged by enemy action in the Second World War and demolished in 1952.

St Mary Matfelon's Churchyard – or Gardens – was renamed Altab Ali Park by Tower Hamlets Council in 1998, in memory of a young Bengali clothing worker from Cannon Street Road, stabbed to death in Adler Street in a racist murder on 4 May 1978. (See page 53 - 55.)

In 1989, as a memorial to Altab Ali and to recognise a turning point in the struggle against racism, the London Borough of Tower Hamlets commissioned Welsh artist and blacksmith David Peterson to make a wrought iron arch for the entrance to the park. The design is based on both Bengali and European architecture, and consists of bands of red coated metal wrapped around and interwoven through a tubular structure.

Poster of Arch unveiling, 1989. Courtesy Alan Dein

The arch built in memory of murdered Altab Ali was unveiled in 1989.

Shahid Minar (Martyr's Monument)

Shahid Minar (Martyr's Monument) is also in Altab Ali Park. It is an abstract work of art – a white structure representing a mother protecting her children in front of a rising crimson sun erected in 1999. This is a locally-made replica of a larger memorial in Dhaka, Bangladesh, which commemorates the 'Language Martyrs' shot dead by the Pakistani Police on 21 February, 1952 during a protest against the imposition of Urdu as Pakistan's state language.

In February 1999, the United Nations declared February 21 World Mother Language Day. At midnight on 20 February (Shahid Dibosh) the martyrs of Language Movement is remembered in a solemn ceremony in the Park and the Bengali community comes to lay wreaths. Abdul Gaffar Choudhury, a journalist and freeman of Tower Hamlets, wrote a Martyr's Day song, *Amar bhaier rokte rangano Ekushe February.* [1]

Shahid Minar, Altab Ali Park. 2010 © Kois Miah/Swadhinata Trust

Tagore

A giant cedar once stood near St Mary Matfelon's foundations. This has now been replaced with a cedar sapling. Embedded in the path, metal letters form a poem by Bengali poet, Rabindranath Tagore, (1861-1941) who won the Nobel Prize for Literature in 1911 and wrote the national anthems of India and Bangladesh: The shade of my tree is offered to those who come and go fleetingly. [2]

Toynbee Hall

Toynbee Hall (28 Commercial St), was founded by local vicar Canon Samuel Barnett, and his wife, (later Dame) Henrietta Barnett, in the early 1880s, as a centre for education and social action in the East End.

The building has impressive political connections. Clement Attlee, MP for Limehouse and Labour Prime Minister from 1945-51 lived here in 1910. The economist Sir William Beveridge planned the principles of the modern welfare state in Toynbee Hall. His work formed the basis for the establishment of the National Health Service and the modern benefits system. Interestingly, Beveridge himself was born in Bengal, India in 1879, the eldest son of a judge in the Indian Civil Service. Toynbee Hall has a long history helping the East End community. In the 1960s the Council of Citizens of Tower Hamlets organised English classes for Bengali seamen and machinists here. Today it continues to serve the Bengali community by providing a meeting place, study centre, lecture hall and base for social programmes and religious, political and cultural events. [3]

Donald Chesworth became Warden of Toynbee hall in 1977. He had been very active in the committee to support Independence in Bangladesh in 1971
(See page 51)

Sonali Bank

The Sonali Bank, on Osborn Street, which can be seen at the start of Brick Lane, is used by Bengali workers to send remittances to their families in Bangladesh. The UK is the fifth largest source of remittances after Saudi Arabia, USA, UAE and Kuwait. Total remittance from the UK to Bangladesh in the fiscal year 2008-09 was US$789 million which is around 9% of total remittance of US$9.69 billion received in Bangladesh.

Brick Lane

Brick Lane probably came into being as a field path east of the boundary of the medieval Priory of St Mary Spital (which was founded even longer ago, in 1197, and which gave Spitalfields its name). The lane was little more than a field path outside the City of London, and acquired its name from the time after the Great Fire of 1666. This was when London clay was extracted from deep pits in the fields, to be fired in smoky kilns to make the bricks needed for rebuilding the city. Heavy carts ferried bricks along the rutted lane to Whitechapel.

The architect, Christopher Wren, was said to have described Brick lane as 'unpassable by coach, adjoining to dirty lands of mean habitations.'[4]

Mina Thakur's Brick Lane Arch dates from 1997 and, like Brick Lane's lamp-posts, is adorned with the crimson and green colours of the Bangladesh flag. Street names are also translated into Bengali script.

The Bangladesh Welfare Association (see Chapter 4, page 50) stands close by in Fournier Street, while the Brick Lane Jamme Masjid, or Brick Lane Mosque stands in Brick Lane itself (see page 59-61).

Brick Lane 1973 – a much quieter, more subdued street than today.
© Tower Hamlets Local History Library and Archives

VIDEO FILM
BOOKS
MAGAZIN
CASSETTE
CD's
ALSO SPECIALIST
PAN

CHEMIST

P L M

PLM
TEXTILE
MERCHANTS
& EXPORTERS

86

B263 FAN

By the 1970s, the former synagogue (on the left with a triangular roof) had become a mosque and, though not easily visible here, the street was already earning its name as the 'Curry Capital' of Europe.
© Tower Hamlets Local History Library and Archives

Other important buildings in the Brick lane area

Police station
Brick Lane police Station opened at 66 Brick Lane E1 on 13 Nov 1978 after demands from the local Bengali community for protection from racial attacks. The current site of the Police Station opened at 25 Brick Lane E1 on 13 Jan 1984.

Police cop it from marchers, 1979 (Press Cuttings Collection, Bishopsgate Library)

The **Montefiore Centre** on Hanbury Street, was established in the 1970s by the Inner London Education Authority.
It was the base for many community initiatives including the Federation of Bangladeshi Youth Organisations.

Chapter 8 - Footnotes

1 Jones, 2004

2 Jones, 2004

3 Jones, 2004

4 Jones, 2004

Chapter 9

Culture and the media

Early cultural activism

During the late 1960s the Bengali Cultural Association promoted cultural activities and produced Bengali dramas in the East End of London including Clive of India and Sirajudd aula. Throughout the 1970s the Bengali Cultural Association produced a number of Bengali plays directed by the late Amar Bose.

Lily Khan and others organised cultural events at the Whitechapel Centre, Myrdle Street, London E1. There were also a number of cultural activists during 1970s. Amongst them were Lutfur Rahman Shahjahan, Laila Hasi, M A Rauf, Oboi Khan, Miftar Ali, Abdul Malik, Kutub Uddin, Asab Ahmed, Rajonuddin Jalal and Ashraf Mahmud Neswar.

Ashraf Mahmud Neswar formed a drama group called the Mitali Arts Group, based at the Whitechapel Arts Centre. Ashraf Mahmud Neswar wrote and directed a number of plays. During this time a number of other cultural organisations were established amongst them were Dishari Shilpi Gosti, Amra Ko Jona, Jhalok Artist Group, Seven Star Drama Society.

A bilingual, in Bengali & English, play "What about Me" performed by Mitali Arts Group, written and directed by Ashraf Mahmud Neswar in 1979. In picture left to right, Ashraf Mahmud Neswar, Gulam Mostafa and Yasmine. Photo: Courtesy Ashraf Mahmud Neswar

Many of the youth organisations formed in the late 1970s organised cultural activities or staged dramas including the Bangladesh Youth Front, the Progressive Youth Organisation and the Bangladesh Youth League.

In the mid 1980s a number of other cultural organisations were established. Bangla Shahitta Parishod in 1985, Sanghati Sahitya Parishod, a poetry organisation was formed in 1989 and Udichi Shilpi Goshti in 1989. A Bengali Drama Festival was organised by Rahman Jilani on behalf of the Asian Studies Centre based at the Toynbee Hall. A significant development took place in the 1980s was the emergence of the Bengali film maker Ruhul Amin. He made many notable films for the BBC and channel 4, most of them documentaries and experimental dramas. His films included "A kind of English" a social drama in 1986 for Channel 4 and Moviwallah, about Bangladesh's film industry in 1993.

Dishari Shilpi Ghosti performing in the mid 1980s. From left to right, Lutfur Rahman, Farzana Salique Shapla and Sabir Ahmed Rolek.
© Dishari Shilpi Ghosti, courtesy of Uchchall Salique

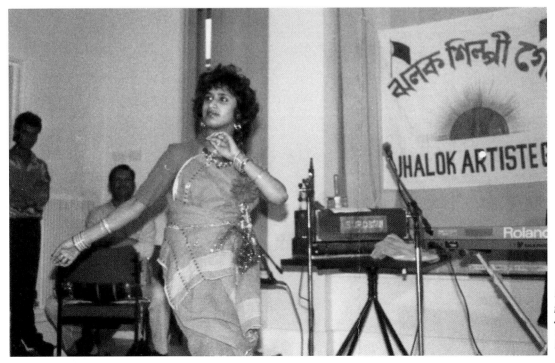

Syeda Lovely Choudhury performing with Jhalok Artist Group in Jagonari, 1989. Photo courtesy Syeda Lovely Choudhury

Black Eagle

In the last 10 years, Brick Lane has become a popular and fashionable area of London and is dotted with clubs and bars playing contemporary club and dance music, but its association with entertainment has a long history. At the sign of the Black Eagle, for example, some of London's hippest nightspots – the trendy 93 Feet East and the Vibe Bar exist in old brewery buildings that can trace their origins to the 17th century.

The Black Eagle brewery was built as long ago as 1669, and was preceded by the Red Lion brewery in Brick Lane. Beer-making in the area at first relied on the pure spring water available nearby, and the skills of the Huguenot brewers. The Black Eagle was purchased by Joseph Truman at the end of the 17th century and beer-making continued until 1988.

The performers performing at today's nightspots include many now well-established Asian mainstream artists who came out of the Asian underground music scene and had their first public exposure in Brick Lane and the many clubs and bars of Shoreditch area.

Asian music is now firmly rooted in Britain, and has broken out into a mainstream audience. Missy Elliot, Madonna, Britney Spears, Bjork, to name a few, have all used samples or have remixed their tracks with British Asian music.

MESSRS TRUMAN, HANBURY, BUXTON & Cos BREWERY.

19th century Brick Lane Brewery. Truman, Hanbury, Buxton & Co Brewery Brick Lane. Aquatint published by J. Moore 1842.
Source: City of London, London Metropolitan Archives

The rise of Asian music

The rise of Asian music started in the 1970s when Biddu, Steve Coe and Sheila Chandra rose to prominence. However, it was not until the late 1980s that British Asian youth first started to create a new musical genre by combining dance music with the music of their parents' generation.

The youth were growing up in an environment of racial violence and political struggle for self-identity while drawing strength from street culture and their Asian roots. They took pride in their music as they could claim it as their own – neither white nor music imported from the Indian sub-continent. The artists who emerged from this period became some of the most successful Asian artists in Britain. They included the Asian Dub Foundation, Joi, State of Bengal and Osmani Soundz amongst others.

Music from the East End: Joi Bangla Crew on the cover of City Limits.

Mumzy

One of the latest pop sensations to hit the mainstream music circuit is Mumzy. With his debut single One More Dance, he sprang onto the scene with an exciting new sound and distinctive urban style. Combining a smooth, soulful vocal style, catchy pop rhythms and clean-cut, urban look topped with his trademark hat, this 25-year-old is the first person of Bengali descent to create such excitement.

As a teenager, Mumzy, who was born and raised in east London, immersed himself into the urban garage scene that gave rise to groundbreaking musicians like Dizzee Rascal. Mumzy has already toured the world with Tiffinbeats, performing for sell-out audiences in Dubai, Canada, Malaysia and India, which has earned him a strong underground fan-base.

Despite the travel and growing success, Mumzy still retains his London roots and continues to live in Plaistow, where he grew up.

Grime Scene

The Bengali youth of London's East End are now involved in a new genre of music. 'Grime' first emerged from Bow, East London in the early 2000s, primarily as a development of UK garage, dancehall, and hip hop. Grime is typified by complex 2-step breakbeats, generally around 140 beats per minute.

The grime scene has opened the doors to many Bengalis, representing Asian Beats and Bass. Artists like Titchiller, Renegade Boy, Naga and many others have come onto the scene. Deshi Movement is another Grime group of young Bengali singers and rappers from Tower Hamlets, they describe their music as fusion of their British and Bengali lives in the UK.

Deshi Movement performing at 93 feet east, 2010
© Swadhinata Trust Photo Ansar Ahmed Ullah

Music, books, CDs, DVDs

In the 1970s Glamour International/Milfa, a small unit adjacent to Naz cinema was one of the first places to sell Bengali music, newspapers and magazines, and it remains a good place to find a wide selection of Bengali/Asian music, films, newspapers and magazines in Banglatown area.

Geet Ghar (Osborn Street), and Sangeeta opened in 1990s, Mira and Modern Book Shop set up in 1974 (previously Brick Lane Music House) in Brick Lane and others in Hanbury Street. The vibrant music pouring on to the streets mingles with recordings of religious prayer further down Brick Lane.

Naz Cinema 1977 © Tower Hamlets Local History Library and Archives

The Naz Cinema, with the record and magazine shop Glamour International just visible to its left, in 1977. Afterwards it became the Café Naz.

Brick Lane Festivals

Since 1996, a street festival – the Brick Lane Festival –
is held in and around Brick Lane and Banglatown on
the second Sunday of each September. Live bands and
performers entertain visitors and the local restaurants
open up stalls on the street for visitors to try their food.
The festival celebrates and promotes the Spitalfields area,
hoping to attract new business and investment.
The general theme of the festival is 'Food, Fashion and
Music' and it brings together the key elements of the
area for which Spitalfields is renowned – the restaurant
and rag trade/fashion industries.

Baishakhi Mela

The calendar now used in Bangladesh was created by
Fatehullah Shirazi in 1584, during the reign of the Mughal
Emperor Akbar. The New Year became known as
Bangabda or Bengali year. It is celebrated all over the
world, in places where Bengali people have made their
home. A Bengali New Year Festival (Baishakhi Mela) has
been organised by local people in Banglatown every year
since 1997. The celebrations in Brick Lane include music,
food and a grand parade.

Baishakhi Mela photo   Mohiuddin Siddique

Cinemas

At one time there were several local Asian film houses in East London. These included the Naz on Brick Lane, Liberty on Mile End Road the Palaseum and the Bangladesh Cinema Hall on Commercial Road. The rise of video shops has led to the closure of them all.

Café Naz at 46 Brick Lane, was where the old Mayfair Cinema, built in the 1930s, stood. In 1950, it became an Odeon, which closed in 1967 and then became the Naz Cinema, showing Bengali and Bollywood films. It was important enough to be visited by Dilip Kumar, the 'Clark Gable' of the Indian film industry and his heroine Vyjayanti Mala and many Bengali singing and film stars. In the 1970s the cinema was the venue for anti-racist meetings and rallies. It is now the Café Naz. It was thrust into the news in 1999, when a car bomb planted by a neo-Nazi named David Copeland exploded outside (Fortunately, nobody was hurt).

Mayfair 1936
© Tower Hamlets
Local History Library
and Archives

Interior of Mayfair
© Courtesy of Cinema Theatre
Association Archive

The Mayfair Cinema – inside and out. It later became the Naz cimema, and then closed (as a cinema) altogether.

Café Naz 1999 © Tower Hamlets Local History Library and Archives

The Naz cinema (formerly the Mayfair), shown above in 1977, eventually became Café Naz. The picture below dates from 1999. In 1999 the bomb left by the Neo-Nazi activist David Copeland went off outside the Restaurant.

Odeon Mile End, Cinema Theatre Association Archive

The Odeon cinema stood on Mile End Road, opposite the tube station, from 1938. It closed in 1972, then became an Asian cinema, Liberty, which, in turn, closed in 1976. Onyx House, designed by Piers Gough, was built on the site in 1986.

© Courtesy of Cinema Theatre Association Archive Palaseum exterior and interior

Courtesy of Cinema Theatre
Interior of Palaseum
© Courtesy of Cinema Theatre
Association Archive

The Palaseum/Essoldo, 226 Commercial Road, is now a site of a supermarket. It opened in 1912 as a purpose-built theatre for Yiddish opera, but became the Palaseum cinema within six months of opening. It then became the Southan Morris cinema and, later, the Essoldo before reverting to the Palaseum in 1966, when it showed only Indian/Bengali films. These pictures show both its interior and exterior.

The Grand Palais, 133-139 Commercial Road, underwent a number of name and use-changes, including New King's Hall, when Lenin spoke there, Imperial Picture Palace and Bangladesh Cinema Hall. It was used as a cinema from 1911 to 1923, then a dance hall, a Yiddish theatre and finally a Bengali cinema before becoming a wholesale clothing shop. In 1969 when Bengali nationalist leader Sheikh Mujibur Rahman came to the UK he was received at the Grand Palais. During the Bangladesh Film Festival, Bengali films are now shown at the Genesis Cinema, which opened in 1999, having previously been the ABC and then the Cannon.

Cinema Theatre Association
Archive Bangladesh Cinema
Hall/New King's Hall/Imperial
Picture Palace/ Grand Palais,
133-139 Commercial Road

The news media

The Bengali population is served by a rich and varied print media, with a long history. It can be traced back as far as 1916, with the founding of Satyavani, a multi-lingual journal, which included Bengali, published in the Strand. In 1926, the Seamen's Bulletin was also published – bilingually, in Bengali and Urdu, from 88 East India Dock Road. The first Bengali weekly journal Jagat Barta was published in 1940 from the Shah Jahan Mosque, Woking. These journals were published to win support of the Indians, especially the Bengali population, in favour of the UK during the first two World Wars, and to accelerate the independence of India. Further journals were published between 1947 and 1971. Until 1970 the main focus of attention of the Bengali community was on Pakistan (as today's Bangladesh was part of Pakistan). In 1971, that focus shifted to Bangladesh.

There are currently more than half a dozen Bengali weekly newspapers, one English-language weekly and two dailies, all published from London. There are also various periodicals regularly published from London and Birmingham. Now there are two 24-hours UK-based Bengali TV channels, three Bangladeshi channels and a number of Bengali radio programmes/stations – Betar Bangla, Radio Bangla on Spectrum (no longer), and Bengali programmes on BBC Network East, Sunrise & on Kismat Radio (no longer), and on Akash.

Correspondents from Bangladeshi and Bengali newspapers based in other countries are also working here.

There are probably more than 200 journalists, performers and technicians working in the UK Bengali media. This number is increasing day by day and, in 1993, the London Bangla Press Club was established to represent and strengthen the relationship among the British Bengali journalists. The offices of Janomot, London's longest running Bengali weekly newspaper are now situated in Chicksand Street. It was first published on 21 February 1969 from 303 Brixton Road, London and moved to its current site in 1991. [1]

© Janomot

The first issue of Janomot.

Kobi Nazrul Centre

The Kobi Nazrul Centre is at 30 Hanbury Street. It is a Bengali arts centre, founded in 1982 and opened by Lord Fenner Brockway. Exhibitions, seminars, concerts and performing arts take place in the beautiful concert space upstairs.

The centre is named after Kazi Nazrul Islam (1899-1976), the national poet of Bangladesh, who produced most of his work between 1920-30. The British administration in India jailed him during the Indian Independence struggle and banned some of his books. A great humanist, he wrote against sectarianism, slavery, colonialism, and for social justice and women's rights.

The Centre was refurbished and re-opened in 2001. Artist Chila Burman came up with design idea after visiting Dhaka and the Kobi Nazrul Centre, and wanted to represent the many facets of Kazi Nazrul Islam's life. It has an etched glass door and the banner (hung in reception) to reflect his colourful dynamic political and philosophical life.

Kobi Nazrul Centre, Hanbury Street. 2010 © Kois Miah/Swadhinata Trust

Opening event of the Kobi Nazrul Centre, 23rd October 1982. Some of the artists performing are: Himangshu Goswami, Kawsar Habib, Mahmudur Rahman Benu, Shamim Choudhury and Habibur Rahman. Photo: Courtesy Ashraf Mahmud Neswar

Chapter 9 - Footnotes

1 Ahmed, 2008

References and further reading

Adams, C., 1987, reprinted 1994. Across seven seas and thirteen rivers. London: 1st edition THAP Books, reprint Eastside Books.

Ahmed, F., 2008. Bengali journals and journalism in the UK (1916-2007). London: The Ethnic Minorities Original History and Research Centre.

Asghar, M.A., 1996. Bangladeshi community organisations in East London. London: Bangla Heritage Ltd.

Ali, Rushanara., 2008. [online] Available at: <http://www.rushanaraali.org>

Ansari, H., 2004. The infidel within, Muslims in Britain since 1800. London: C. Hurst

Anwar, M., 1979. The myth of return: Pakistanis in Britain. London: Heinemann

Balfour-Paul, J., 1998. Indigo. London: British Museum Press.

Balfour-Paul, J., 1997. Indigo and the Arab world. Richmond: Curzon

Basu, Shrabani., 2003. Curry – the story of the nation's favourite dish. Stroud: Sutton.

Bangladesh Support Group. 2010. [Online] Available at: <http://www.basug.nl>

Bangabandhu Primary School. [Online] Available at: http://www.bangabandhu.towerhamlets.sch.uk/

Banglapedia. [Online] Tea http://www.banglapedia.org/httpdocs/HT/F_0107.HTM

Bettington, C., 2003. Exploring the vanishing Jewish East End. London: LB Tower Hamlets

Birnbaum, B. Eversley J. Clouting T. Allard, D. Hall, J. Woods, K. Allen R & Tully D., The clothing industry in Tower Hamlets – An investigation into its structure and problems in 1979/80 and beyond. London: Queen Mary College and LB Tower Hamlets Mimeo).

BritBangla 2002–3. [Online] Available at: <http://britbangla.net/honorary.html>

British Library. [Online] Available at: http://www.british-library.uk See especially: British Library. Help for Researchers: Asians in Britain: Ayahs, Servants and Sailors [Online] London. Available at: <http://www.bl.uk/reshelp/findhelpsubject/history/history/asiansinbritain/ayahsservantsandsailors/britishayahs.html>
See sections on:
Marine Department Records (L/MAR/C/902, vol. 1, ff. 25-26)
Records of the Economic Department, L/E/7/1152, file 727;
Report of the Conference held at the India Office, 22 February 1923
and: <http://www.bl.uk/onlinegallery/features/trading/events1.html>

Burton, A., 2003. Janaki Agnes Penelope Majumdar. Oxford: Oxford University Press.

Cadbury, Helen (2010) Sailing to Britain: The Education Resource Pack, London, TARA

Callaghan, J., 1993. Rajani Palme Dutt: A Study in British stalinism. London: Lawrence & Wishart.

Carey, S., 2004. Curry capital: the restaurant sector in London's Brick Lane. London: Young Foundation.

Chalmers, R., 1996. Learning Sylheti. London: Centre for Bangladesh Studies.

Choudhury, Y., 1995. Sons of the empire. Birmingham: Sylheti Social History Group

Choudhury, Y., 1993. The roots and tales of the Bangladeshi settlers. Birmingham: Sylheti Social History Group.
Chowdhury, M.R., 2001. Sylhetis in the UK. London: Siloti Translation & Research Centre.

Collingham, L., 2006. Curry – a tale of cooks and conquerors. London: Vintage.

Commonwealth War Graves Commission. [Online] Available at: http://www.cwgc.org/search/cemetery_details.aspx?
cemetery=90002&mode=1

Communities and Local Government. [Online] Available at: <http://www.communities.gov.uk>

Connections: Hidden British histories. [Online] Available at: <http://www.connections-exhibition.org>

Crang, P., 2005. Fashioning diaspora space: textiles, pattern and cultural exchange between Britain and South Asia
1850s-80s, 1980s-2000s. London. Royal Holloway, University of London. [Online] Available at: <http://www.diasporas.ac.uk/
casestudies_archive.htm>

Crill R., 2002. Indian textiles in Georgian Britain http://www.bl.uk/onlinegallery/features/trading/events1.html

Crowe A.L., 1956. Josiah Child and the EIC. Ph.D. University of London

Department of Communities and Local Government., 2009. The Bangladeshi Muslim community in England –
understanding Muslim ethnic communities. London: DCLG

Eade, J et al., 2006. Tales of three generations of Bengalis in Britain. London: Nirmul Committee.

Fisher, M., 2006a. Working across the seas: Indian maritime labourers in India, Britain, and in between, 1600–1857,
International Review of Social History. 12/2006. [Online] Available at: <http://journals.cambridge.org>

Fisher, M., 2006b. Counterflows to colonialism: Indian travellers and settlers in Britain 1600-1857. Delhi: Permanent Black.

Fisher, M, Lahiri, S & Thandi, S. 2007. A South-Asian history of Britain: four centuries of peoples from the Indian
Sub-continent. Santa Barbara: Greenwood World Publishing.

Fryer, P. 1984. Staying power: The history of black people in Britain. London: Pluto Press.

Fishman, W, 2006. The streets of East London. Nottingham: Five Leaves Publications.

Globalising Art, Architecture and design history. 2004. [Online] Available at: <http://www.glaadh.ac.uk>

Greater London Authority., 2006. Muslims in London, London: GLA.

Greater London Authority., 2009. ONS mid-2007 ethnic group population estimates. GLA DMAG. [Online] Available at:
<http://www.lho.org.uk/viewResource.aspx?id=15248>

Greater London Trade Union Resource Unit., 1985. Black workers and trade unions. London: SERTUC.

Griffiths, J., 2007. Tea: the drink that changed the world. Andre Deutsch.

Griffiths P., 1979. A history of the joint steamer companies. London: Inchcape & Co. Ltd.

Griffiths P., 1977. A History of the Inchcape Group. London: Inchcape & Co. Ltd.

Griffiths P., 1974. A licence to trade: the history of English chartered companies. London: Ernest Benn Ltd.

Griffiths P.Y. 1967. The history of the Indian tea industry London: Weidenfeld and Nicholson.

Grove, P, & Grove, C. 2009. Curry and spice and all things nice: the what - where – when. [Online] Available at: <http://www.menumagazine.co.uk/book/book.html>

Grove, P. 2008. What do aromatherapy and curry have in common? [online] Available at: <http://www.menumagazine.co.uk/book/book.html>

History of 'Indian' restaurants and curry houses in Britain. [Online] Available at: <http://www.resthof.co.uk/history.htm>

Huque, M., 2009. The story of East End Community School. Dhaka: Mohammed Ishaque

Indian Catering. London. [online] Available at: <http://www.indian-catering.co.uk/indian-caterers.htm>

Indian Government Report., 1947. Our merchant seamen. Modern India Series 3. Delhi

Islam, N., 1989. Probashir Katha, Sylhet: Probashi Publications.

Jagonari Women's Education Resource Centre. [Online] Available at: http://www.jagonari.org.uk

Jones, D., 2004. Exploring Banglatown and the Bengali East End. London: LB Tower Hamlets

Kobi Nazrul Primary School. [online] Available at: http://www.kobinazrul.net/

Kajol, Ishaq (2010) The Tea Workers movement of Surma valley, Dhaka, Ittadi Grantha Prokash

Knott, K. and Roche, K. 2005. Disaporas, migration and identities. [online]. Available at: http://www.diasporas.ac.uk/

Lamarche, D., 2003. Bengalis in East London – a community in the making for 500 Years. London: Swadhinata Trust.

Lenman, B., 2001. England's colonial wars, 1550-1688. Cambridge: Pearson.

Lenman, B., 2006. The World of the East India Company. Boydell Press/National Maritime Museum.

Lichtenstein, R., 2007. On Brick Lane. London: Penguin Books.

Lipman, V., 1954. Social History of the Jews in England 1850 - 1950. London: Watts & Co.

Macfarlane, A. & Macfarlane, I. 2003. Green gold: the empire of tea. London: Ebury Press

Matar, N., 1998. Islam in Britain 1558–1685. Cambridge: Cambridge University Press.

Michael Madhusudan Dutt 1824-1873. [Online] Available at: http://www.enotes.com/nineteenth-century-criticism/dutt-michael-madhusudan

Momen, A, et al. Occupation 84. 2009. [Online] Available at: http://www.occupation84.org.uk/index.htm

Morris, D., 2007. Mile End Old Town 1740–1780. London: East London History Society.

Moving Here: 200 years of migration in England. [Online] Available at: <http://www.movinghere.org.uk> See especially: Tracing your roots [online] Available at: <http://www.movinghere.org.uk/galleries/roots/asian/ukrecords/lascars.htm>

London. This is the source for Section XXIII of the Merchant Shipping Act Amendment Act, 1855 18 and 19 Vict. c. 91, which is available in the National Archives under reference (PRO)MT 9/650 (File M 15609 / 1900)

Mukherjee, S., 2010. Nationalism, education and migrant identities: the England-returned. London: Routledge.

Office for National Statistics. [Online] Resident Population Estimates by Ethnic Group June 2007 Available at http://www.neighbourhood.statistics.gov.uk/dissemination/LeadPage.do?pageId=1005&tc=1275906986098&a=7&b=276772 &c=tower+hamlets&d=13&e=13&f=21810&g=346968&i=1001x1003x1004x1005x1007&l=1809&o=198&m=0&n=6286&r =1&s=1275906986098&enc=1

Old Bailey. 2010. The proceedings of the Old Bailey, 1674-1913 [online] Available at: <http://www.oldbaileyonline.org/browse.jsp?id=t17650227-5-defend86&div=t17650227-5#highlight>

Pereira, C., 2008. The view from Shooters Hill: the hidden black and Asian history of Bexley. London: BACCA

Plummer, A., 1972. The London Weavers Company 1600–1700. London: Routledge and Kegan Paul

Public Advertiser. 1785. Letters column. London: 16 March 1785. No 15854.

Ragged School Museum, A history of London's East End communities. [Online] Available at: http://www.raggedschoolmuseum.org.uk/nextgen/history/localareahistory.shtml

Rahman, Urmi (2010) Bilete Bangali, Dhaka, Sayitya Prakash

Renton, P., 2004. The lost synagogues of London. London: Tymsder Publishing.

Report from the Committee on lascars and other Asiatic seamen, Parliamentary Papers, 1814-15, Vol. III, No 471, pp.4-5

Restaurant Hall Of Fame. 2008. [Online] Available at: http://www.resthof.co.uk

Robins, N., 2006. The corporation that changed the world: how the East India Company shaped the modern multinational. London: Pluto Press.

Sanaton Association 2007 London. [Online] Available at: <http://www.sanaton.org.uk/>

St Matthias Community Centre. 2009. History of St Matthias Old Church Poplar. [Online] Available from: <http://www.stmatthiascommunitycentre.com/history.jsp>

Shapla Primary School, 2008. [Online]. Available at: http://www.shaplaprimary.co.uk

Sherwood, M., 1991. Race, Nationality and Employment among Lascar Seamen 1660 - 1945. New Community, Vol 17(2) : 229-244 (January)

Sherwood, M. 2007 Lascar struggles against discrimination in Britain 1923 – 1945: the work of N J Upadhyaya and Surat Alley. [Lecture].

Sherwood M, & Tasneem, S., 2008. Bangladesh armed forces [Article] in 37th anniversary transforming Bangladesh: a commemorative publication. London: Bangladesh High Commission.

Social Exclusion Knowledge Network. (2007). Understanding and tackling social exclusion. final report of the Social Exclusion knowledge Network of the Commission on Social Determinants of Health. Geneva, World Health Organization; USDA Foreign Agricultural Service Bangladesh Cotton and Products Annual (2009) Available at: http://www.apeda.com/TradeJunction/Report/APRIL_2009/Bangladesh_Cotton_Products_Annual.pdf

Sokoloff, B., 1987. Edith and Stepney - The life of Edith Ramsay. London: Stepney Books.

South Asia citizens web. [Online] Available at: <http://www.sacw.net>

Taj Stores. 2006. A Brief History of Taj Stores. [Leaflet] published for 70th anniversary. London.

Taylor, R., 2004. Walks through history: exploring the East End. Derby: Breedon Books.

Time Out, June 6-12, 2007, No 1920, p 150 [Online] Available at: <http://www.timeout.com>

The Ships' List. 2007. The Fleets: C.W. Cayzer & Company / Cayzer, Irvine & Company / Clan Line of Steamers Limited / Clan Line [online] London. [Online] Available at: <http://www.theshipslist.com/ships/lines/clan.html>

Tower Hamlets London Borough. Black history walks in Tower Hamlets (Walks 4 and 5). [Online] Available at: www.towerhamlets.gov.uk

THHOL. The black and Asian presence in the Tower Hamlets [online] Available at: <http://www.mernick.org.uk//thhol/miscellany01.html>

Ullah, A. 2008 The Bengali community and the docks – the role of lascars. Paper presented on a study day titled 'The Docks, Empire and Slavery' at the Museum in Docklands, 14 June 2008.

University of Leeds, 2005. Diasporas, migration and identities. [Online] Available at: <http://www.diasporas.ac.uk/>

Visit East London.com [Online] Available at: <http://visiteastlondon.com>

Visram, R., 1986. Ayahs, Lascars and Princes: Indians in Britain 1700-1947. London: Pluto Press.

Visram, R., 2002. Asians in Britain – 400 years of history. London: Pluto Press.

Wemyss, G. 2008. White memories, white belonging: competing colonial anniversaries in 'postcolonial' east London. Sociological Research Online, Volume 13, Issue 5, London Goldsmiths, University of London. [Online] Available at: <http://www.socresonline.org.uk/13/5/8.html>.

Wemyss, G., 2009. The invisible empire – white discourse, tolerance and belonging. Surrey: Ashgate.

Zaman, S., 2003. Mirza Shaikhite Samuddin and his travelogue: Shigurfnama I Velayet. London: Shams N. Zaman

Appendix 1

Time Line

1600	East India Company founded
1614	First record of Bengali settlement in London
1617	Mughal trade treaty with East India Company
1648	The East India Company moves its headquarters to Leadenhall street
1690	The East India Company establishes a new base in Calcutta, Bengal
1757	Annexation of Bengal by East India Company
1764	East India Company defeats an alliance of Mughals Bengal & Awadh at Buxar
1765	Robert Clive acquires the management of the Bengal treasury for the East India Company
1773	Norris Coffee House serves curry in Haymarket London
1801	First lascars hostel is opened
1806	Opening of new East India Dock
1802	Ayahs' home established in Aldgate
1856	The strangers home for Asiatics, Africans and south sea islanders built in West India Dock Road
1858	UK Parliament replaces East India Company with direct British rule in India
1874	The dissolution of East India Company
1895	M M Bhownaggree – an Asian – becomes MP for Bethnal Green
1914-1918	Thousands of lascars play crucial role in both the Merchant Navy & the Royal Navy during the First World War
1920	The first Indian restaurant in east London is opened
1939-1945	Lascars worked on British Naval ships & in the Merchant Navy in large numbers. Many settled in Britain after war.
1947	Indian independence and the partition of India, with Pakistan, a largely Muslim state comprising East Pakistan (now Bangladesh) and West Pakistan
1951	Pakistan Welfare Association founded
1970	the Awami League, under Sheikh Mujibur Rahman, wins an overwhelming election victory in East Pakistan. The government in West Pakistan refuses to recognise the results, leading to the independence movement
1970	Tosir Ali killed by racists in Aldgate
1971	Bangladesh Liberation War
1976	Brick Lane Jamme Masjid (Brick Lane Mosque) opened
1978	Ishaq Ali killed by racists in Hackney
1978	Altab Ali stabbed to death in Whitechapel
1982	Kobi Nazrul Centre established
1986	Jagonari Women's Educational Resource Centre opens
1989	Altab Ali arch unveiled in park at Whitechapel
1997	First Baishakhi mela (Bengali new year fesival) held
1997	Brick Lane and surrounding area branded 'Banglatown'
1999	Shahid Minar (martyrs monument) erected in Altab Ali park
2001	Spitalfields ward named Spitalfields & Banglatown ward

Appendix 2

Many accounts of the arrival of the Bengali seamen talk about them arriving in the 1950s. However as Michael Fisher has shown, Asian seamen (not only Bengalis) arrived -and not all left - in steadily rising numbers from the middle of the eighteenth century.

Asian seamen arriving in Britain, 1760-1855.

Year Reported arrivals that year

1760 138

1780 167

1796-1814 Approximately 2,500 lascars settle in Britain (source Cadbury)

1803 224

1804 471

1805 603

1806 538

1807 1,278

1808 1,110

1809 965

1810 1,403

1811 929

1812 1,193

1813 1,336

1814-1815* 1,000-1,100

1821-1822 509

1855* 3-3,600

* Estimates
Taken from Fisher (2006a), p.36